Barbara Forisha-Kovach

THE
FLEXIBLE
ORGANIZATION

A Unique New System for
Organizational Effectiveness
and Success

A SPECTRUM BOOK

Prentice-Hall, Inc., Englewood Cliffs, New Jersey 07632

214306

658.4
F721

Library of Congress Cataloging in Publication Data

Forisha-Kovach, Barbara.
    The flexible organization.

    "A Spectrum Book."
    Includes index.
    1. Organizational effectiveness.   2. Organizational
change.   I. Title.
HD58.9.F67 1984   658.4'06   83-24591
ISBN 0-13-322321-3
ISBN 0-13-322313-2 (pbk.)

10 9 8 7 6 5 4 3 2 1

ISBN 0-13-322321-3

ISBN 0-13-322313-2 {PBK.}

Editorial/production supervision by Elizabeth Torjussen
Cover design © 1984 by Jeannette Jacobs
Drawings by Kathryn Mundus Steinaway
Manufacturing buyer: Pat Mahoney

This book is available at a special discount when ordered in
bulk quantities. Contact Prentice-Hall, Inc., General
Publishing Division, Special Sales, Englewood Cliffs, N.J. 07632.

Prentice-Hall International, Inc., *London*
Prentice-Hall of Australia Pty. Limited, *Sydney*
Prentice-Hall Canada Inc., *Toronto*
Prentice-Hall of India Private Limited, *New Delhi*
Prentice-Hall of Japan, Inc., *Tokyo*
Prentice-Hall of Southeast Asia Pte. Ltd., *Singapore*
Whitehall Books Limited, *Wellington, New Zealand*
Editora Prentice-Hall do Brasil Ltda., *Rio de Janeiro*

Contents

Preface

In the past several years, American corporations have been forced by economic circumstances to examine their foundations and to build new structures to guide a process of organizational change. The desired outcome is increased organizational effectiveness. The process of change has been one of both despair and hope, of individual deprivation and individual opportunity, of organizational failure and organizational success. The result may well be a reshaping of the American industrial complex, with widespread ramifications for all other areas of our society.

This book is the product of my own involvement in the process of organizational change. I have worked with colleagues for several years to develop a new approach to studying people in organizations. Much of the theory and research that support this work is presented in the book *Organizational Sync* (Prentice-Hall, Inc., 1983), a forerunner of this one. As we have developed theory and conducted research, however, we also have been involved with the *process* of change in major corporations. In our work with management and supervisory units at Michigan Bell Telephone, National Broadcasting Corporation, Ford Motor Company, and General Motors Company, we have helped groups of managers conceptualize their own change process, establish goals, and implement plans to guide that process. We have learned as much from them as they have from us—perhaps more—and this book is largely a result of those experiences.

The book itself contains as many pages of examples, exercises, and charts as it does of actual text. For some readers, it may serve as a manual for exploring the change process within their organizations. For others, it may provide another way of understanding the process of organizational change as it affects their own lives. It is my hope that all readers may find in the book a new vantage point from which to look at some part of their individual experiences within organizations. Perhaps a few readers will also find specific material that will give them the know-how to assume control over the process of organizational change in their own work environment.

Many individuals have contributed, some unknowingly, to the process of developing this book. Individuals in my class in organizational psychology at the University of Michigan–Dearborn—most of whom work in corporate settings—have provided much insight into the effects of change in individual lives. Supervisors and managers in corporations with whom we have had an ongoing work relationship have allowed us to share part of their experiences; thus, shaping, altering, and giving substance to our own viewpoint.

Long theoretical discussions with various individuals over many months also sharpened the ideas presented in this book. For challenging the thesis of this book from their own perspective I am grateful to Nancy Badore, Ph.D., of Ford Motor Company and professors Tom Lyons and Dick Krackenberg of the College of Management, University of Michigan–Dearborn. Other less extensive discussions with Wendy Coles of General Motors and Jeff Walters of Ford Motor Company have also contributed to this book. Although these people may not support all of my conclusions in this work, their insight and knowledge were important to its development.

My greatest debt of gratitude, however, goes to my associates at Human Systems Analysis, Inc.—those who have shared the process of theoretical development, research, and application. Patricia Kosinar of Eckerly Corporation in Boston has been a continuing source of support and dialogue as we discussed theory and application of organizational theory and practice. Glenn Morris of Hillsdale

College, Dow Conference Center, has been an integral part of my experience in organizations and also a contributing partner in both theory and application. Finally, my husband and cofounder of Human Systems Analysis, Randy Kovach, is in many ways more responsible than I am for seeing this work, as well as all others, through to conclusion and for providing the larger understanding of organizational behavior within which our concepts and models have been formulated and tested.

I must acknowledge as well the many others without whom our organizational work could not continue: Tim Artist and Jim Kruz, who have produced superb videotaped portraits of managerial training; Helen Linkey and Jim Dallaqua, who have processed quantities of research data; Ann Handrinos, who has filled in behind a videotape camera, drawn charts and graphs, and helped with the research; Bill Bardallis, who has provided the computer programming; and Helen Morrison, who has been a continuing source of advice and support.

In our own work, all of us have had to learn how to work together as part of an effective team and to recognize strengths and limitations in ourselves and others. One of the messages of this book is that increased effectiveness in organizations depends upon the degree of effectiveness of groups and teams within that organization. If this book helps others to become part of—or to create—effective teams in their workplaces, then it will have met its purpose well.

1
Organizational Effectiveness and the Management of Change

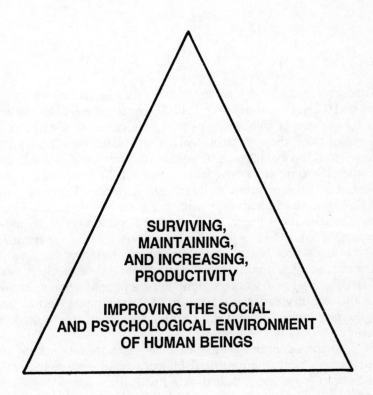

SURVIVING,
MAINTAINING,
AND INCREASING,
PRODUCTIVITY

IMPROVING THE SOCIAL
AND PSYCHOLOGICAL ENVIRONMENT
OF HUMAN BEINGS

American organizations are in trouble. More Americans are unemployed than at any time in our history. The headlines of almost any daily newspaper give examples of the difficulties of the American economy as a whole. A giant steel mill in Buffalo, New York, shuts down and leaves 10,000 employees on the street out of work. The automobile companies have laid off over 250,000 workers, many of whom will never return to their jobs. American Telephone and Telegraph, slowly acting to meet the demands of governmental deregulation, is giving many workers the option to relocate, move down, or leave the company. Universities, social service agencies, and public school systems are retrenching in the face of significantly lower funding. In some areas, the number of laid-off teachers rivals that of laid-off auto workers. Soup lines, a phenomenon unknown in this country for nearly 50 years, are forming in Detroit, and volunteer groups around the country are organizing to feed the needy.

At the same time that many businesses are retrenching and others are closing, there is astonishing growth in some sectors of the American economy. Although faced with fierce competition, IBM grew by $5 billion in sales in a single year. United Technologies, a staid and stolid aircraft engine maker, has grown to be a multibillion dollar conglomerate, building elevators, air conditioners, and semi-conductors while still holding on to the lion's share of the jet engine business. Johnson and Johnson, set back on its heels by a madman poisoning its headache remedies in Chicago, responded quickly and smoothly to apparent disaster, and within weeks the Company regained most of its market share.

Even among those organizations in trouble there have been remarkable instances of staying power, growth, and productivity. Redoubled efforts on the part of the employees of a Michigan steel plant kept the plant open long enough for a successful buyer to be found, and the days of threatened closure are over. We all know that Lee Iacocca brought Chrysler back from the brink of disaster, eking a small profit margin out of the pages of red ink. Ford made news as well last year for cementing a major management-union agreement based on employee involvement that may be part of an effort to turn a profit next year. And General Motors, the giant of the automobile companies, has posted a profit for the second straight year.

Organizational Effectiveness

What accounts for the tales of success and the tales of failure? The answer, in part, is that our world has changed a lot in the last five to ten years. Organizations are coping with a new economic environment in which resources are scarcer and competition is fiercer than ever before. They are coping as well with the customer's response to this new environment, which is to demand quality and economy instead of status and style. However, the new environment is only part of the answer.

The other part of the answer can be found within the companies themselves—not only in the products they sell, but in how they are produced, marketed, and sold. The winners—the money tree companies—know how to organize their people better than the losers. They know how to organize their people to respond quickly and smoothly to a changing environment. They match the changing environment with a flexible organizational structure that is in touch with current conditions. Successful organizations know how to cope with change.

In short, organizations that are effective today, and those that promise to be effective tomorrow, are those that have the ability to change in response to a shifting social and economic environment. The key to organizational effectiveness today is not unyielding strength but flexible resiliency. The old analogy of the oak that blows over in the wind where the bamboo reed bends and stands up straight again is applicable to our situation. What was certain yesterday is uncertain today. What were accepted practices before are missing the mark in our current situation. What worked in the past leads to disaster in the present. Such a situation demands that organizations view changing circumstances as opportunities for refining goals, reevaluating objectives, and increasing productivity in directions that meet the needs of a new reality (see Figure 1.1). Organizations must change, despite the slow and painful process of change—and often they emerge stronger.

FIGURE 1.1
EFFECTIVE ORGANIZATIONS IN TIMES OF CHANGE

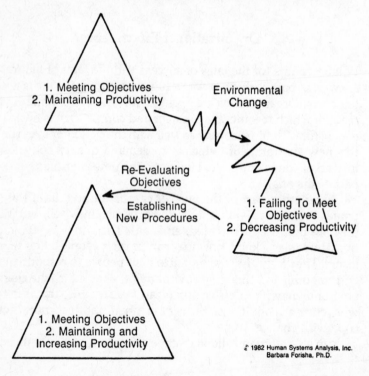

1. Meeting Objectives
2. Maintaining Productivity

Environmental Change

Re-Evaluating Objectives

Establishing New Procedures

1. Failing To Meet Objectives
2. Decreasing Productivity

1. Meeting Objectives
2. Maintaining and Increasing Productivity

© 1982 Human Systems Analysis, Inc.
Barbara Forisha, Ph.D.

The Nature of Change

Americans have historically been a people who believe in change and in adventure. Change has often been viewed as meaningful merely for the sake of change. However, as our country has grown from adolescence into maturity, its people have developed a stronger attachment to stability and the status quo. We like things the way they are—or the way they were—and are reluctant to face the prospect of a revolution in living and working. Further, if we are forced to change, we wish to do so instantly, and get the transition over all at once. Coming out of our societal adolescence, we still tend to dream about instant transformations in which the old gives way to the new overnight. Genuine change, however, in both people and institutions is slow, complex, and incremental (see Figure 1.2).

Change as a slow process.   Events that instigate change in human affairs may at times appear sudden, shocking, and abrupt. Mt. St. Helens did erupt overnight; the merger of Stroh's and Shafer's was celebrated in one day; and the deregulation of AT&T became a fact at the start of 1983. But even apparently sudden changes are themselves often years in the making. And for human beings to absorb these kinds of changes, and to create patterns that respond appropriately to them, will take much longer than one day or one night. Permanent change in people and systems takes place only over time. The process of transforming the old into the new occurs by fits and starts and is not complete until individuals and systems have integrated and stabilized new patterns of behavior. The effects of such change—and the benefits—may be apparent only after a year or more has passed.

For example, the official act of signing a merger may precede by years the former employees of one company trusting and respecting the former employees of the other company. The deregulation of major utility companies may not affect the practices of many managers reared in the good old days, when the style of management was different. Slowly, such managers may opt for change or early retirement, yet they will influence company practices for years to come. Some major corporations may have arrived at new philosophies of decision-making practices, and even may be successfully implementing more participative procedures in some instances, but others still remain "telling" organizations, where bosses tell employees what to do and expect not to be questioned or challenged.

FIGURE 1.2
THE NATURE OF CHANGE

1. SLOW

Events which instigate change may be abrupt but genuine.

Change which integrates new patterns of expectations and behavior occurs only over time.

2. COMPLEX

Change in any part of a system affects all other parts.

3. INCREMENTAL

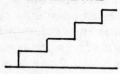

New behaviors are learned and integrated one step at a time with much trial and error along the way.

Changes in the human systems trail behind changes in official organizational documents and executive policy. Individuals change slowly, and systems composed of many individuals change even more slowly.

When Bob Thomasen, a supervisor in an engineering division of a manufacturing company, attended a training program, he developed some new patterns of behavior. As he began to apply this behavior in the workplace, his employees became suspicious of the motives for this change. Bob had always been an authoritarian so-and-so, bossing his people around. Now he was asking them for their opinions (even though he always gave them a five-minute lecture after they responded) and occasionally he told a joke and

6

stood around with his men on the floor. His employees wondered what was going on. They wondered if he was setting them up—and consequently set him up by coming in late and not putting equipment away. When he responded in his old dictatorial way, they smiled and said, "See, he hasn't changed at all." But Bob had changed, and after this outburst, he redoubled his efforts to develop a style that involved his employees more often. One year later, Bob and his employees have developed a new level of trust for each other—and the department is much more participative than formerly. Change occurred—but only over time did new patterns of behavior become a stable part of the human system.

Change as a complex process.   We all live in overlapping systems where individuals are interdependent with many others. Change in one part of a system affects all the other parts. Most of us, for example, are part of organizational systems where we not only work in one unit but also may belong to a committee or a task force. Both are systems in themselves. Then we may also live in families, and we have circles of friends and community associations. Tension generated by changing the leadership of one committee may affect our performance on the task force as well as work in general. We may bring this tension home to our family, where our family members may spread it to the rest of their associations as well as our own.

When Bob Thomasen began to change his behavior at work, the changes affected not only his immediate employees but his family as well. Just as he had always told his workers what to do, he also had always told his wife and children what to do. His family, just as his employees, had been used to the old obnoxious behavior. Suddenly they were puzzled, confused, and uncertain. His children wondered if something was the matter with Dad. Ultimately, they too had to learn some new behaviors.

Additionally, the change that was occurring in Bob's work unit impinged on another work unit. As Bob Thomasen's employees got themselves together with his new style of behavior, their unit became more effective. The second unit watched from the sidelines. This other group had always been the leader in productivity and had regarded itself as a model of organizational effectiveness. As the men in this work group watched Bob's unit take hold, they became disgruntled and began telling Bob's employees that this was all a con job on Bob's part and that they should not listen. Their challenges to

Bob's employees were passed on to Bob. Only when Bob persisted in his new ways, and persuaded his employees to do the same, did the second unit begin to accept that something new was happening. Slowly, some of the changes spread into the second unit, and after a year or so, the changes that Bob had begun were finally accepted practices.

Bob's unit was closely connected with only one other unit. If it had interfaced with a number of other units, changes in Bob's department would have been even more difficult. Changing large systems involves more complexity—and takes more time—than changing small ones. The changes must overcome the roadblocks of each area as new groups take account of the changed behaviors.

Systems change that involves behavioral changes inevitably lead to changes in procedures, roles, and production methods. Over time, behavior has been codified in rule books, and as behavior changes, so must all the rules that govern behavior. In each organizational area, established ways of doing things have been written down in policy booklets, with the weight of the past often measurable by the amount of organizational paper that has accumulated on the subject. Change throughout a system, therefore, often means discarding or rewriting the rulebooks of the past that legitimate those behavior patterns.

Change as an incremental process.   Change happens one bit at a time. The acceptance of new behavior on the part of one individual does not happen overnight. The implementation of new behavior between divisions of a major corporation may begin with enforcing the letter of the law in one small section on the order forms sent back and forth between divisions. If this new practice is established, and over time increases the effectiveness of the two units' interaction, other ways to increase effectiveness may also be agreed upon. The first steps in change often seem small and insignificant but are the stepping stones for later activities of larger scope. The acceptance of Quality Circles in a manufacturing setting begins with the success of one circle, so that others see the results and want to be successful too. Within a year or two, there may be a great many successful Quality Circles within that setting.

Just like learning to walk, change proceeds one step at a time. In another way, too, change can be compared to toddlers learning to walk. Toddlers fall down a lot because they have not quite got the hang of this new behavior. As individuals and systems experiment with new behaviors, they are bound to make mistakes, to be clumsy in implementation, and to do things poorly. Effective behavior requires practice and is perfected only slowly. When Bob Thomasen finally learned to smile, he said he felt as if his smile were cracking his face. In fact, it looked rather like it was, but he got better over time. Effectiveness comes with practice. Consequently, in systems change there are many ups and downs as new behaviors, procedures and policies are implemented, reevaluated and often redesigned until they are flowing in harmony with each other.

The Paradoxical Nature of Change

At each step along the path of change there are both opportunities and limitations. Not only is change slow, complex, and incremental but it is also paradoxical. The forces of change eradicate old ways of being at the same time as they create opportunities for new and more constructive ones. The loss of old ways of being is almost always experienced as painful although there may be excitement in the possibilities that open up. Individuals caught in the throes of change thus experience their worlds as both contracting and expanding at the same time. They are required to adjust to the necessities of retrenchment and the imperatives for innovation at the same time (see Figure 1.3).

One of the administrative officials at the University of Michigan commented in the midst of the recession of the early 1980s that we seemed to be living a schizophrenic existence. On the one hand, we would spend four hours in a meeting deciding which units and sometimes which faculty were going to be cut back in order to meet new budget requirements; and, on the other hand, we would go to another long meeting to explore new possibilities for university facilities and faculty to contribute to the corporate community. We would cut back old programs and start up new ones which promised greater productivity down the road. The juxtaposition of the cutbacks and the expansion was sometimes enough to make a person's head spin. It is often difficult to live with both at the same time.

However, it is only possible to take advantage of the opportunities afforded by changing circumstances if individuals are willing to live with both retrenchment and innovation simultaneously.

FIGURE 1.3
THE PARADOXICAL NATURE OF CHANGE

Shrinkage	VS	Expansion
Retrenchment	VS	Innovation
Loss	VS	Opportunity
Adaptation	VS	Leadership

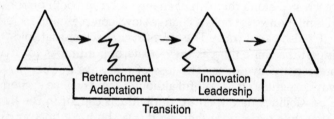

Retrenchment
Adaptation

Innovation
Leadership

Transition

The demands of retrenchment cannot be ignored, and we must turn our attention to them. It is our choice, however, whether or not we choose to make use of the opportunities as well. If we fail to do so, then we will know only the pain of change—the sense of giving up something important—and ignore the possibilities for growth. Our world will contract and possibilities narrow.

However, if we meet the demands for letting go of what has been and creating what will be at the same time, we are able to shape the course of change. Retrenching under pressure is adaptation. Creating a new course is leadership. In times of instability and uncertainty, the leaders who arise will adapt to overwhelming forces and shape new directions—both at the same time.

Focus on Process

The leaders who emerge to shape future directions will be those who understand the nature of change. Change is a process and not a product. Living in transition requires that individuals focus on how things are done and not what is to be accomplished. The results of any change process may only be assessed after time has passed. In the meantime, rewards for individuals and organizations will come from handling the process well and from creating organizations that respond to the challenges of change. Succeeding in such a time means, in fact, living in the meantime, for individuals in uncertain times experience themselves as neither here nor there, but rather as in between.

For each individual and each organization, therefore, *how* business is transacted in the coming years will be of paramount importance. How do you respond to change? How do you create flexible organizations with structures appropriate for present purposes? What directions do you give up? Which do you pursue? For any given individual in an organization, the answers to these questions are determined by the strengths that emerge in the interplay of personality and organizational climate. A knowledge of one's own personality and an understanding of one's organization are the tools with which an individual may shape the process of organizational change. All who have a hand in shaping this process are the leaders of tomorrow.

In summary, organizational effectiveness will be increased by those individuals who:

1. Understand the function of different organizational structures and their corresponding climates;
2. Know their own personality style and recognize that of others;
3. Develop their own management style to the fullest and assume leadership responsibilities;
4. Work well with others and are able to reconcile conflicting viewpoints;
5. Are clear in expressing their own point of view and good at drawing out the viewpoints of others;
6. Recognize and strengthen the constructive expectations of their group and organization;
7. Make decisions from the widest base of information and implement these decisions;
8. In doing all the above, shape the process of organizational change as we move from the past through the present into the future; and
9. Use the tensions accompanying change as motivation for personal growth and success.

Each of these areas will be the focus of one of the chapters that follow. The emphasis throughout the book is on the importance of individual leadership in achieving organizational effectiveness. The by-product of working toward stronger organizations is often personal success.

EXERCISE: PROBLEMS AND OPPORTUNITIES IN CHANGE

1. List some of the problems that you see arising in your organization because of recent changes in the economic environment.
2. If possible, discuss with others in your organization the items that you have listed. Can you agree on three items that present the greatest problems or carry the greatest risks for your organization?
3. For each of the items you listed state at least one way in which each problem presents new opportunities for the organization.

2
Organizational Structures: Balancing Pyramids and Circles

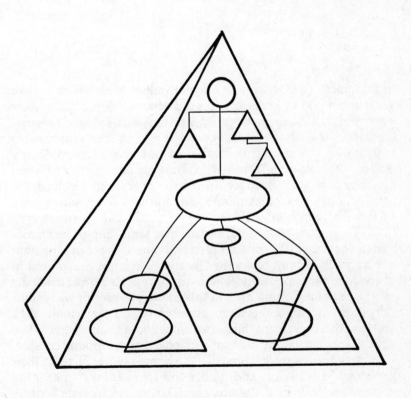

In our reluctance to seek out new opportunities, we are all rather like a certain not-too-bright actor. This out-of-luck fellow could neither sing nor dance in a town that thrived on musicals. Driven to desperate measures at last, he sold his contact lenses and his hearing aid to pay for singing and dancing lessons. At the next audition, a slightly deaf director told him, "Dance when I hold up one finger; sing when I hold up two." Unable to see the man's fingers from the stage, the actor danced when commanded to sing and sang when commanded to dance. Another audition followed with a director who had laryngitis. "Dance," he whispered, and the man sang. "Sing," he hissed, and the man danced. Turned down both times, the man sank onto the sidewalk in front of another theater. Staring at the ground in despair, he gave up his quest, believing once again he had made the wrong decision. Behind him, in this theater, a director was frantically screening applicants for an actor who could dance in the dark and sing through a loud thunderstorm without being distracted by either . . . and still the man sat and looked at the ground outside.

American organizations, like the actor, need to increase their repertoire of behaviors and, unlike the actor, learn to match the appropriate behavior to the situation. The first is important because organizations require a wide variety of available responses to adapt to unpredictable demands from a changing environment. The second is critical because matching the right response to the situation determines the success or failure of the organization.

Increasing the Range of Alternatives

How do organizations increase the range of available alternative behavior and possibilities? Alternatives are increased when (1) organizations encourage all their employees to generate ideas and alternative solutions to possible situations, and (2) they have developed the systems and procedures with which to implement action when an alternative is selected. In other words, organizations need to be able to think, to plan, and to act from the widest possible base of information.

Most organizations do not have a history of meeting each of these needs equally well. Rather, they tend to fall into one of two camps, emphasizing either the importance of generating ideas *or* acting, rather than a combination of the two. Many industrial giants, for example, have failed to encourage their employees to generate ideas to solve current problems. On the other hand, many governmental, educational, and social service institutions have not developed the implementation systems to act on ideas with appropriate speed. In both cases, organizations fail to respond with maximum flexibility to current environmental exigencies.

Selecting the Right Alternative

In order to produce the most successful outcome, organizations must (1) have a thorough knowledge of the problem and the possible consequences, and (2) have individuals in decision-making capacities who can filter and evaluate this information within the largest possible frame of reference. They need to know as much as possible about the situation, including both human and technological factors, and they must be able to think about what they know within a systems-wide perspective, which includes an awareness of the past and possibilities for the future.

Effective decisions are based on information. Organizations in times of change need to know what is happening in the wider world, what is occurring within their own system, and what the possible reactions of human beings within that system may be to various courses of action. This means that they need excellent communication systems. First, they require as many individuals as possible to act as sources of information to report on both external and internal events. They need, therefore, to encourage individuals who have access to information to look, to listen, and to share this information with others. Second, they need to create channels of communication within the organization so that all available information flows toward the individuals in decision-making capacities. In many organizations, this means opening upward channels of communication, often blocked by fear and protocol.

Once the information is gathered, organizations require individuals in decision-making capacities who can filter and evaluate this information. These individuals are those who can take both a wide and long view. They can assess incoming information in terms of the total system, balancing potential effects on individuals against effects on the system, weighing the effects on one unit in contrast to others. They must be able to assess this information in terms of past history and possible consequences. They must be able to assess both short- and long-term results of immediate action and strike an effective balance between short- and long-range gain. Finally, they must be able to act—and accept the consequences of their action. An outcome is never guaranteed and every decision entails the risk of failure as well as success.

Structures and Climates

The potential for developing all of these behaviors is increased when organizations create a variety of formal and informal organizational structures. Different structures generate different climates within organizations and promote different sets of individual expectations. Organizational climates are, in fact, collective sets of individual expectations. When individuals expect that their information, ideas and opinions will be accepted, they are more willing to contribute to the corporate pool of knowledge. When individuals expect that their ideas will be heard by those at the top, they are more willing to pass their knowledge upward. When individuals expect that their information makes a difference and affects courses of action, then they become better information gatherers and selectors themselves—and often more productive human beings.

To simplify, we are suggesting that specific organizational structures (whether codified in organizational charts or exemplified in patterns of human relationships) generate certain climates. Organizational climate is both a result of and an influence on individual expectations. Individual expectations guide human behavior. Expectations that the organization is both receptive to ideas and able to act upon those ideas will generate greater individual productivity and organizational effectiveness.

Pyramids and Circles

What structures then will lead to maximum productivity and effectiveness in times of change? We have conceptualized the necessary structures as pyramids and circles, with their corresponding climates, and argue that organizations are most effective when they have created the appropriate balance between the two to meet the needs of their own goals and situations (see Figure 2.1).

Pyramids are hierarchical systems of organization, with a few power wielders at the top and many followers at the bottom. Pyramids symbolize power and the task dimensions of organizational activity. They are designed for accomplishing tasks and getting things done. *Circles,* on the other hand, are flat and all members are relatively equal. They do not have hierarchies to differentiate member status, but rather generate expectations that everyone's opinion carries equal weight. Circles symbolize affiliation, or the human dimensions of organizational activity. They are designed for people to share information and ideas and to provide self-confirmation for individual members.

Pyramids are effective for making final decisions and for implementing action plans. Individuals at the top of pyramids who have been receptive to information from throughout the system have the capacity to see the ramifications of decisions on all units over time. From this position, they can also monitor the actions of individuals in various roles as they implement action plans. There are certain benefits to viewing situations from the top—the visibiilty is greater and details are placed in the larger context.

Circles, in contrast, are effective for gathering information and for generating alternative courses of action. Structurally, circles lie

17

FIGURE 2.1

FUNCTIONS OF PYRAMIDS AND CIRCLES

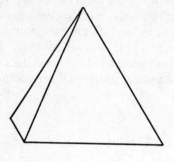

PYRAMIDS are Appropriate for
• Accomplishing Specific Tasks
• Implementing Accepted Procedures
• Doing Things Quickly

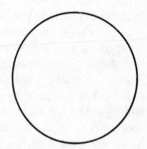

CIRCLES are Appropriate for
• Clarifying Ambiguous Situations
• Creating Lists of Alternatives
• Winning Acceptance for New Ideas

flat against the ground and have more points of contact with their environment. They are able to absorb more information than the taller pyramid, which is more concentrated on up-and-down channels of information than on those that flow in and out. Circles are also effective for sharing ideas and generating alternatives. Individuals within circles are regarded as equals, so that individual contributions are valued and considered on their merits. The flat structure of the circle encourages the sharing of information, the formulating of possibilities, and the valuing of human beings.

The climates generated by pyramidal and circular structures are quite different. Effective pyramids are characterized by efficiency, briskness, and a sense that things are happening. Effective circles are characterized by openness, warmth, and responsiveness to individuals. Pyramids encourage people to work hard and get things done. Circles encourage people to share their ideas with each other and to imagine new possibilities.

In times of change, many organizations seek to incorporate both structures within the overall organizational system. Many pyramidal structures are seeking balance by introducing circles. Some more circular organizations are introducing pyramids. As institutions attempt to create a balance within themselves, they are experiencing all the difficulties that occur in any period of transition (see Examples 2.1 and 2.2).

Example 2.1 A Pyramidal Organization

One major manufacturing corporation, traditionally tall and skinny as the Eiffel Tower, has recently been propelled by increasing losses to reevaluate its own structure. Those at the top have made the decision (in their customary autocratic manner) to flatten their organization and to develop circles at all levels of the corporation. Although circles *have* been introduced into the corporation and the span of control increased at all levels, old ways die hard. Managers still tell other managers what to do and these managers tell their subordinates. Subordinates keep their ideas to themselves from fear of reprisals for unwanted suggestions. The process of opening up communication channels and generating new ideas among employees at all levels has begun—but the process of actually implementing the new ideas will take many years.

Example 2.2 A Circular Organization

One division of a public utility company has long been an organization dominated by circles. The primary function of this division is to generate new ideas for marketing the company's product. In the past, the division has been very effective in the marketing area. Personnel within the division have been encouraged to be creative and innovative. In the middle 1970s, this division became part of a Quality of Work Life effort. They instituted formal circles in which employees could discuss their work and suggest solutions for problems. The QWL philosophy fit with that of the division, and there was an easy and smooth transition from the informal to the formal circular structures. This division recently, however, has become part of a deregulated national utility organization and has entered a competitive market. The change has shaken the division, which is now developing a new model for employee behavior. As one manager said, "We all used to wear our QWL jackets. Now, we're supposed to take them off, and become 'tough managers.'" Emerging into a competitive arena, this company is now seeking to build some pyramids amidst its circles, so that their company can prosper in a competitive world.

Establishing a Balance

When effective pyramids and circles exist within organizations they are likely to be more effective as total organizations. They have the capacity to gather information, generate alternatives, select courses of action, and implement action plans. They have available to them the widest range of possible behaviors. The exact balance of pyramids and circles will depend on the overall goals of the organization and its current situation, but each organization requires such a balance.

The flat circular structures absorb information from the environment and generate alternative possibilities in terms of this information. Individuals within circles develop a sense of belonging to the organization and experience themselves as influencing the course of the organization. As a consequence, ultimate decisions will engage the acceptance and commitment of individual members. The hierarchical, pyramidal structures within the organization will then use this information, evaluate a wealth of alternatives, and make final decisions and monitor implementation. Within the pyramidal structures, roles will be defined and responsibilities assigned. Operating, however, from a circular base, decision makers may be confident that their decisions will be generally accepted— because all will have had an opportunity to have input into the decision.

Lack of Balance

A scarcity of either pyramids or circles within an organization hampers its effectiveness. In stable economic times, the lack may be relatively unnoticed. In unchanging circumstances, continuous communication with the external environment is less necessary, since yesterday's information will do as well as today's. Consequently, pyramids can survive without circles. Similarly, in a stable situation, innovative, difficult, and rapid decision making is less often required, since yesterday's procedures may serve as guidelines for today's actions. Thus, circles can survive without pyramids. However, in turbulent times, when much is unknown and familiar patterns are no longer viable, the lack of either effective pyramids or circles may promote a rigidity of behavior which cannot adapt to changing circumstances.

The rigidity of behavior that results from an imbalance of pyramids and circles may be symbolized by two new structures: crooked pyramids and squishy circles (see Figure 2.2). Pyramids that stand alone in a shifting landscape lack the information and employee support to respond to rapidly changing circumstances. In self-defense, such pyramids, shuddering as the ground shifts, bend over and become crooked. As they bend, they dominate their employees, repressing innovation and new ideas.

In similar fashion, circles that stand alone in times of change lack the ability to make difficult decisions and to implement them rapidly. In the face of failure, such circles begin to draw in their boundaries, demanding that the appearance of the organization be

FIGURE 2.2

INEFFECTIVE PYRAMIDS AND CIRCLES

Dominate Subordinates
Control Behavior
Repress Innovative Ideas

CROOKED PYRAMIDS

Avoid Conflict
Control Behavior
Limit Information Flow

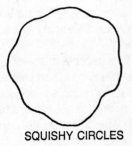

SQUISHY CIRCLES

preserved at all costs and that employees draw even closer together. Like the out-of-balance pyramid, as the circle contracts, it begins to control its members by requiring that they stay together, avoid conflict, and give the appearance of unity and agreement. Becoming crooked and squishy is a response to a need for certainty. By contracting their shapes, organizations may appear to gain some security in tightening the boundaries that separate them from an uncertain world.

Opportunities in Turbulent Times

Security is not found in contraction but in expansion and innovation. If organizational structures open themselves to their environment and become more aware of current and forthcoming changes, they gain more information on which to base decisions about their future course. Pyramidal organizations that incorporate circles and circular organizations that grow pyramids will have the greater flexibility with which to respond to crises in their environments. The alternative that offers the greatest chance of survival is not contraction but innovation, not closing in but opening up, not becoming crooked and squishy but upright and round both at the same time.

What this means is that individuals in pyramids, threatened by changes in their environment, will increase their effectiveness by welcoming and choosing among the very ideas that are threatening to them. The changes that are instigated by the environment require that *they* adapt to this new environment, by incorporating many of the ideas that might have been foreign to them before. On the other hand, individuals in circles, bewildered by new demands for economic efficiency, may survive by considering some new structural alternatives, by reallocating power among hierarchical task forces, and balancing these new hierarchies with their traditional circles.

The process of seeking a balance between pyramids and circles is one that is required by the forces of change. The process requires that past behaviors be evaluated and new behaviors be established. The process of choosing a future course, moreover, will give rise to new leadership. As new courses are selected, those who are willing to participate in their selection will move to the forefront of organizations. The mantle of leadership will fall on these who can create new directions—and not on those who rigidify the directions of the past.

The Process of Leadership

Those individuals who are excited about new opportunities to create functional balances within organizations are as excited about the *process* that is occurring as they are about the *end product* that might result. They are enthusiastic about what is going on at the moment and are not solely focusing on what the ultimate rewards will be. In their ability to involve themselves in the present process, they are the ones who will shape the future. Those who adhere to the past and constrict their systems within rigid structures will wither away as the old yields to the new. Those who focus only on the future and the end product create another kind of rigidity, for they are constrained in the present by the boundaries of their future visions. They will never make it into the future that they envision, for they are not giving enough attention to the road that leads that way.

Leaders have both vision and direction. They envision what may come and choose their directions in terms of their images of what will be. Once they do so, however, they focus on the process of getting there and give their attention primarily to the present, thriving on the immediate challenge. Ultimately, even though they have chosen the course and established the goals, they may be surprised at the results that do emerge. They are similar to travelers on a train who have selected their destination but then are so taken with the other occupants of the car and the scenery outside the window that arrival at the desired location takes them unaware. To lead in times of change means to focus as much on the process as on the final product and to profit from the adventure of being en route and living in between.

EXERCISE: MINI-ORGANIZATIONAL
EXPECTATIONS INVENTORY

Instructions

In the box or circle next to each statement, write a number from 1 to 4. In my organization this:

4—always or almost always happens.
3—often happens.
2—occasionally happens.
1—rarely or never happens.

People are selected for jobs because they:
- _____ ■ know people in the organization.
- _____ ■ are friends with the boss.
- _____ □ have essential skills.
- _____ ○ can work within and shape the system.
- _____ □ have the right credentials.
- _____ ○ have growth potential.

People are advanced in the organization because they:
- _____ ■ are willing to listen.
- _____ □ agree with those in power.
- _____ □ have privileged information.
- _____ ○ create an effective network.
- _____ ■ are available at all times.
- _____ ○ develop their own replacements.

Approaches to planning include:
- _____ ■ never giving up on problems.
- _____ □ spelling out duties in detail.
- _____ ■ everyone having a part in decisions.
- _____ ○ establishing priorities.
- _____ ○ seeking the best advice from all sources.
- _____ □ one person making decisions.

Organizational beliefs include:
- _____ ■ different leadership styles are accepted.
- _____ □ everything must go through channels.
- _____ □ tasks are assigned from the top.
- _____ ○ diverse talents are used effectively.
- _____ ■ information is available to everyone.
- _____ ○ people perform in areas where they do best.

People want to work because they:
- _____ ■ enjoy being with others.
- _____ ■ want to keep their boss happy.
- _____ □ want to get a better title.
- _____ ○ want to make a contribution.
- _____ □ enjoy being in charge.
- _____ ○ want to make a contribution.

Scoring:

To identify your perceptions of your organization, first add up all the numbers in the plain boxes. Then add up all the numbers in the shaded boxes. Subtract the plain box sum from the shaded box sum, multiply your answer by 2 and then divide by 5.

You perceive your organization as a Pyramid if you scored less than −2

You perceive your organization as a Circle if you scored more than +2

You perceive your organization as a Cone or Combination of Pyramids and Circles if you scored between −2 and +2.

Then add up all the numbers in the circles.

If your score is more than 30 you perceive your organization as effective

If your score is less than 20 you perceive your organization as ineffective

If your score is between 20 and 30 you perceive your organization as effective in some areas and ineffective in others.

(For further information on the interpretation of your scores see *Organizational Sync.*)

3
Personality Styles and Individuals in Organizations

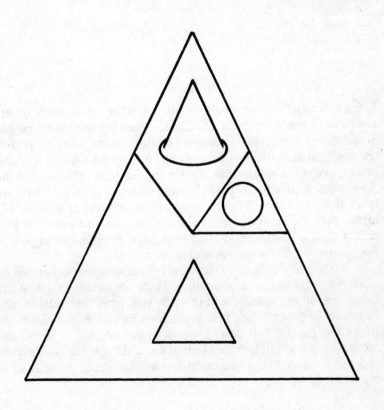

Some individuals always walk slowly down the street, while others rush, out of breath, to leave the current place behind. Some people arrive at new ideas while staring out of the window, feet propped on the desk, amid a clutter of papers and coffee cups. Others are most productive when they sit intently in a quiet orderly office, feet on the floor, chair square to the desk. Most of us know managers who are loud and forceful and others who are warm and accepting. We know, too, many employees who are precise and punctual and others who are lackadaisical and impulsive. People, like organizations, come in many shapes and sizes.

In the last chapter, we discussed the *expectations* generated by different organizational structures. These expectations guide the behaviors of individuals within each structure. Individuals also have sets of expectations that guide their behavior. Individual expectations parallel our description of organizational expectations. Moreover, a good fit between individual and organizational expectations increases the productivity and satisfaction of individuals in organizations.

Personality Styles

Some people's expectations tend to take a *pyramidal* form. Such individuals expect that the world—and its organizations—will operate in a logical, hierarchical fashion focused on getting things done. Other people's expectations take a *circular* form. They expect that people in general will operate in a more intuitive modality, respecting the value of human beings and focused on sharing information and experiences with each other. Still others balance these two sets of expectations and shape their expectations in a *conical* form, recognizing the importance of both hierarchical and flat modalities, and the necessity of both getting things done and sharing with others. (See Figure 3.1.)

Those whose expectations are mostly pyramidal we call *Producers.* Producers, who make up the bulk of our world, assume that the world is shaped like a pyramid, with a few on the top and many on the bottom. They base their behavior on this expectation. They respect the authority of those above them, and use their own authority to tell those beneath them what to do. They rely on logic and proven procedures. They sometimes believe that if all schedules, procedures, and timetables were clearly enforced, the world would be an efficient—and comfortable—place in which to live and work.

Those whose expectations are mostly circular we call *Processors.* Processors make up only a small part of the population. They view the world as a circle, with everybody equally valuable to the functioning of the whole. They base their behavior on this world view. They tend to value the opinion of most people, and they often bypass the channels created by organizational authorities in order to share information with other individuals. They rely on intuition and sometimes ignore proven procedures. They believe that if all individuals were respected for their potential contributions, the world would be a warm—and productive—place in which to live and work.

Those in between, whose expectations are shaped in both pyramidal and circular forms, and whose expectations may be symbolized by the cone, are called *Integrators*. Integrators make up approximately one-third of the population—and the bulk of the managerial population. They view the world as an alternating landscape of pyramids and circles and, in their own behavior, seek to

FIGURE 3.1
CHARACTERISTICS OF PERSONALITY STYLES

	PRODUCERS (50%)	INTEGRATORS (35%)	PROCESSORS (15%)
	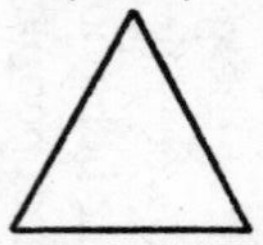 △	 ⊿	 ○
Primary focus of Attention:	Requirements of System	Requirements of System & Needs of Individual	Needs of Individual
Area of Creativity:	Products	Systems	Ideas
Response to Change:	Resistant	Moderately Open	Open
Willingness to Risk:	Low	Moderate	High
Style of Thought:	Logical	Logical & Intuitive	Intuitive
Preferred Activity:	Doing	Planning	Thinking

maintain a sometimes precarious balance between the two. They rely alternately on logic and intuition, being neither as logical as Producers nor as intuitive as Processors, but seeking to bring the two together into a working balance. They tend to believe that maintaining a balance between individual contributions and established procedures will provide the greatest flexibility for an efficient and caring world.

Personality Styles and Organizations

Each of the personality styles—Producer, Processor, and Integrator—is necessary to maintain the effectiveness of an organization. Producers are *doers,* relatively content to carry out the routine business of the institution. Their relatively large numbers parallel the need for their orientation in maintaining the day-to-day effectiveness of any workplace. Producers are needed at almost all entry-level positions of organizations, and higher up in the accounting, engineering, and technical hierarchies. (See Example 3.1.)

Example 3.1 Description of a Producer

Don Adamson, a 55-year-old engineer, is chief executive officer of a division of 5,000 salaried employees. His early years were spent in the navy, where he rapidly assumed positions of command. Training at Annapolis and the War College gave him a grasp of good managerial skills. He believed in making decisions at the top—but sharing them with his men. He believed in keeping his hand on the tiller, which was *his* job, and depending on his men to do theirs. Even as he maintained control, however, he spent a lot of time with his men—previously on board ship and now on the plant floor. "A good manager always visits his troops," is a byword with him.

Mr. Adamson is a Producer. He is not instinctively warm toward others—but he has learned that he must share with others. He was not particularly receptive to others' ideas—but he has learned to be fair and consistent and consequently does give his employees a hearing when they wish to talk to him. He treats his employees as equally as possible—holding them all to the same rules and regulations. Mr. Adamson is generally respected and admired by his employees. He has learned the rules of good management and holds himself to these rules, just as he holds others to those that apply to them.

Processors, in contrast, are *thinkers,* and prefer to spend their time generating ideas. Often limited to certain areas of the organization, they thrive on the opportunity to create new ideas and envision new directions. Their relatively small numbers are sufficient for the needs of most organizations, where maintaining the procedures of the past is necessarily more important than generating future directions. The work of Processors, however, is vital and they are generally found at higher-level positions in marketing, research, and training and development. There are few entry-level positions for Processors. (See Example 3.2.)

Example 3.2 Description of a Processor

Tom Barker is a 45-year-old manager of an engineering unit. His upward rise as a young researcher had been stalled by his unwillingness to play by the rules of the large industrial company. Consequently, in midcareer, he received a lateral move to a managerial position over 65 men. Although this position entailed considerable responsibility, there were few chances of promotion and was regarded internally as a de facto demotion. In managing his unit, Mr. Barker relies on his own sense of intuition. He responds to some of his employees more warmly than others, but he responds to all of them. He likes being with people, and often closes the day sitting in his own or a subordinate's office, reviewing the day—and possibly the fishing conditions for the next weekend.

Mr. Barker is a Processor. He is receptive to people, likes to discuss new ideas, and chooses to operate on "what feels right" at the moment. Conceptually, he is in touch with the "big picture," but concretely, on a day-to-day basis, he sees what and who is before him at the moment. Mr. Barker is both loved and hated. Those whom he spends time with love him. Others, who are unintentionally ignored in the rush of the day, hate him. They assume that he is "out to get them." Rather, Mr. Barker simply hasn't run into them—nor thought of them—as he goes about his business. Although he tries to be consistent in his behavior with his subordinates, his good intentions generally fade away, and he lapses into companionable discussions with those whose offices adjoin his. At such times, he is likely to excuse his behavior by reminding himself that "consistency is the hobgoblin of small minds."

Integrators are *planners,* intent on building the structures for both Producers and Processors. They choose the present course, using the lessons of the past and imagining the possibilities of the future. In organizations, Integrators often move toward the top of each hierarchy, as they delight in making things work from a systems perspective (see Example 3.3).

Example 3.3 Description of an Integrator

Renata Christensen is head of a troubleshooting unit for a worldwide manufacturing organization. She has just turned 40 and is one of the youngest people at her level in the entire corporation. Her rise in the company since she finished a master's degree (in an unrelated field) has been very rapid. She is highly thought of by all the people she works with, from the president of the corporation down to the hourly workers with whom she has come in contact.

Ms. Christensen is an Integrator. She is warm and responsive to others, but only within the limits that are set by her corporation. She does not indulge in long conversations with single individuals—unless business is involved—but is always willing to listen (for a while) to anybody who comes to her door. Many people in the company go to talk to Ms. Christensen regularly—and leave feeling comforted.

Ms. Christensen is always aware of the larger goals that she has set out for herself, working toward a better future for the organization as a whole. She balances the needs of individuals with those of the system. She understands the "big picture" of her corporation, but sometimes makes her decisions in light of pressing individual needs that come up suddenly.

Careful not to overcommit herself, she still sometimes finds herself tired and overworked. Her Integrator's style extends beyond the workplace, where she is still seeking to balance her commitments in her work and personal life.

Personality Styles and Change

Each personality style responds differently in times of change. Producers are resistant to change, as they are most comfortable in the patterns of yesterday. They respond to change by contracting rather than expanding. Fearful of losing what they have, they fail to focus on potentials for innovation. In times of change, Producers will be more effective if they are protected from ambiguities by being given new, appropriate procedures and modes of operation. Guided through the process of change without stretching their capacities beyond their limits, Producers will then emerge again as the mainstays of their organization when it stabilizes.

Processors, on the other hand, come to the fore during times of change for they thrive on ambiguity and uncertainty. They view change as an opportunity for sloughing off the past and exploring an ever-promising future. Envisioning new worlds, they may outline the directions to be followed in times of turbulence and uncertainty. Once having outlined the directions, however, they will rely on others to plan the journey and create the road maps. Then, having arrived at a new destination, they will once again be looking toward the horizon as others are focused on the task of building the present.

Integrators tread the path between the Processors and the Producers. Alive to new ideas, they also want to know if the ideas are viable. Aware of the productivity of past methods, they choose with care those that must go to make way for new directions. Integrators may be envisioned as building the bridges between the past and the future, between established procedures and new orientations, and creating the systems within which systems and individuals may make the transition from the old to the new. Not as resistant to change as Producers, nor as open as Processors, they carefully assess the costs and potential gains of both the past and future and create the system which operates most effectively in the present.

Adaptation and Growth

When times are uncertain, individuals may not have the choice of remaining comfortably in familiar patterns. Rather, they are offered two choices: to become less or more than they have been. In times of change, each style has a tendency to emphasize its own characteristics to the exclusion of others. Just as pyramids tend to become more pyramidal (eventually becoming crooked), and circles become more circular (eventually becoming squishy) in the face of change, so the personality styles tend to constrict and become more single-focused in the face of uncertainty. Producers may retreat by emphasizing their control over others by application of rules, regulations, and procedures. Integrators may retreat by emphasizing their own achievement. Processors may retreat into endless talk. Becoming more like one is already is the adaptive response to change. But it is also choosing to contract and become less than one is. This response

34

ignores the possibility of developing new ways of being to suit the new environment.

In times of change, however, the three personality styles may choose to grow, by expanding to incorporate in their own behavior some of the strengths of the other styles. Producers may find a new satisfaction in increasing their awareness of others and learning to share with each other in a team setting. Integrators may better use their talents by not focusing on individual achievement, but rather on using their knowledge and insight to help others achieve, assuming the responsibility for the direction which many others may pursue. Processors may move from their emphasis on interaction with others to a new focus on achievement, putting their ability to talk to work and actually creating what they have been thinking about. (See Figure 3.2.)

Each of these choices is open. The degree of individual insight—and determination—will guide the ultimate course of the individual.

Managerial Responsibility and Personality Styles

Recognizing the choices open to different personality styles in times of turbulence and uncertainty, managers may help shape the course of their peers and subordinates. Knowing that Producers will become more effective by increasing their understanding of human relations, they may create circles for their Producer employees, encouraging them to share their concerns and problems with others. Aware too that Integrators will become most effective in positions of influence, they may allow their Integrator subordinates to exercise their growing managerial competencies within defined spheres. Finally, astute managers may encourage their Processor employees to leave talking behind and to achieve, by granting them the autonomy and providing the resources with which they can do so.

Another way to say the same thing is to talk about motivational strategies for each of three personality styles. Producers become more effective, not when procedures are tightened and controls are imposed, but when they have an opportunity to work and share with others. Integrators increase their own scope, not when they are left to their individual achievements, but when they are given the

FIGURE 3.2
PERSONALITY STYLES AND RESPONSE TO CHANGE

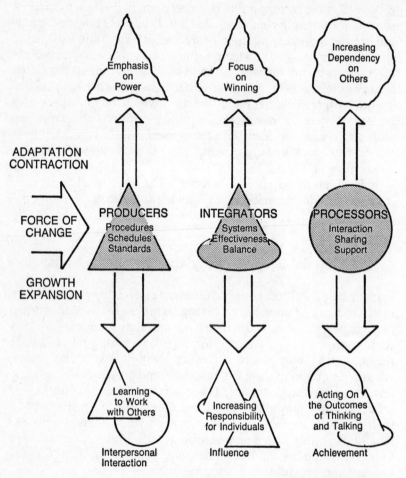

© 1982 Human Systems Analysis, Inc.
Barbara Forisha, Ph.D.

charge to influence and take care of others. Finally, Processors will achieve a higher level of effectiveness when they are led from talking about ideas to doing something about them, and to achieving at high levels.

Such motivational strategies work in times of stability as well as in times of choice. In stable times, however, individuals have a comfortable middle road. Producers will simply *do*, Integrators *plan*, and Processors *think*. However, in times of change nothing is simple. Producers tend to increase the constraints of their power structure—unless they are led or lead themselves to focus on the needs of human individuals. Processors tend to talk without conclusions—unless they learn to focus on getting things done in terms of individual achievement. Finally, Integrators in such times tend to focus on individual achievement—unless they are encouraged to use their talents for the good of the entire system, taking responsibility for the functioning of the whole rather than the part.

Individual Opportunities in Times of Change

Just as our organizational structures, each individual style is required to become more than it is in times of change—or it will inevitably become less. Change does not allow a middle road. Individuals will climb uphill or roll back down, for the comfortable resting place has been lost in the crumbling earth. Each style has its own growth direction. Each direction, moreover, leads to a greater balance as individuals incorporate some of the behaviors and some of the expectations of the other personality styles. In times of change, balance becomes a necessity. Whether in organizational or individual systems, balance produces a greater flexibility which is more adaptable to changing circumstances. In developing this flexibility, however, individuals and organizations not only adapt to change, but they shape the directions of the future which will emerge from the uncertainty of the present.

EXERCISE: MINI-PERSONALITY EXPECTATIONS INVENTORY

Instructions:
In the box next to each statement, write a number from 1 to 4. Mark your answers according to the following scale:
   4—I almost always agree with this statement.
   3—I often agree with this statement.
   2—I occasionally agree with this statement.
   1—I rarely or never agree with this statement.

_____ □ Details are usually unimportant.

_____ ■ The more you learn, the more there is to know.

_____ □ It's hard to know what others are thinking.

_____ □ You can't tell what others expect from you.

_____ ■ Even in a group, people remain individuals.

_____ □ Too many points of view only lead to confusion.

_____ □ There is a right and a wrong way to do every-thing.

_____ □ When things go wrong, it's hard to understand why.

_____ □ It's difficult to try when people keep criticizing you.

_____ □ Some kinds of people just can't work together.

_____ □ Most people share some of the same feelings.

_____ □ Everybody is after the same thing.

_____ □ Everyone should know and follow the rules.

_____ □ There is only one good solution to any problem.

_____ ■ The most important part of making a choice is accepting the consequences.

_____ ■ It's enjoyable to meet and talk to new people.

_____ □ Others don't seem to understand me.

_____ ■ Good problem solving requires hearing differences of opinion.

_____ □ There is no point in changing something that already works.

_____ □ It's good not to decide until you have all the facts.

_____ ■ Careful analysis usually reveals a pattern.

_____ ■ It's good to ask for help when you have a problem.

_____ □ There is little you can do to change the big things in life.

_____ □ First impressions are usually right.

_____ □ Conflict is best avoided.

_____ ■ What each individual does makes a difference.

_____ □ Trusting others is danger-ous.

_____ □ Good teams are made of similar kinds of people.

_____ ■ It's good to hear different points of view when making a decision.

_____ □ They've either got it or they haven't.

_____ □ A good decision keeps all options open.

_____ ■ Even good decisions need to be reevaluated over time.

_____ □ People who get ahead step on others.

_____ ■ It's good to try out different ways of doing things.

_____ □ If it can't be done right, it's not worth doing.

_____ □ Ambition only reflects greed.

Scoring:

To find your personality style, first add up all your numbers in the plain boxes. Then add up all your numbers in the shaded boxes. Subtract the plain box sum from the shaded box sum and divide your answer by 3.

You are probably a Producer if you scored less than −2.

You are probably a Processor if you scored more than +2.

You are probably an Integrator if you scored between −2 and +2.

(For further information on the interpretation of your scores see *Organizational Sync.*)

© 1984 Human Systems Analysis, Inc.

Management
and Leadership Styles
for Organizational
Effectiveness

Keeping one's hand on the tiller is different from sighting the distant horizon. Maintaining one's course in the present is different from envisioning the new lands of the future. Each of these suggests the differing functions of managers and leaders. Managers make the most of the current situation, often seeing that goals are accomplished when it would appear that resources are inadequate for the purpose. As one executive joked, his talents would be superfluous if his unit had plenty of everything. Leaders take people toward a future destination, encouraging others to leave the familiar situation for unknown shores. Management requires the effective supervision of a work unit, no matter what size. Leadership requires the ability to envision, make strategies, and plan what the work unit will do years later—and establish present goals in that context. Management and leadership are sometimes demonstrated by the same individual—and sometimes not. Both are subjects of this chapter.

In times of change, both management and leadership become complex. The structures of organizations that are adapting and expanding with turbulent conditions increase in complexity. Individuals motivated by the forces of change will grow to new levels.

Managing in times of change requires managers to constantly keep in touch with current developments, to open up their own communication network, and to reevaluate past designs in terms of present conditions. To lead in such a time requires not only establishing a firm base on shifting ground, but imagining the contours of the landscape in future times. To both manage and lead, one must be quick on one's feet—and willing to live with uncertainty.

Each personality style—Producer, Processor, and Integrator—has more or less ability to accommodate to uncertainty. Each personality style, however, does have the ability to manage—and some of each style have the ability to lead. The ways in which they manage, however, will be different. Drawing on its own strengths, each management style will create a different climate for subordinates within the organization. From different sets of expectations of the world, each management style will cast a different shadow, creating the employee's world within different outlines.

Yet just as the environment changes, so do managers and leaders grow and change over time. Learning from experience, effective managers mature, creating a more balanced image of the world than when they began. They move from an early single-pointed focus to a more encompassing one, increasing their effectiveness as they do so. Mature managers have developed the inner flexibility that allows them to manage effectively in a changing environment. From their numbers will come the leaders of organizations who will cast their shadows into the future, shaping what is to come.

Producers as Managers

Producers begin as managers by acting as *Chiefs* with reins of authority in their hands. They follow the directions of those above and expect that their own directions will be followed by those below them. They direct others in one-to-one confrontations, in conferences, in meetings and by memos. Their view of the world is such that there are few contingency plans for lack of compliance with directives from the top. (See Example 4.1.)

As Producers mature, however, they become more benevolent and recognize the value of human interaction in making an operation work. They relate to their employees in a warm way—often as a

43

Example 4.1 Producers and Managers: Chiefs

Art Hanson is a 55-year-old supervisor who learned a long time ago that if you want people to do something, you tell them to do it. If they don't do it right away, you tell them louder. Consequently, Mr. Hanson has a reputation for barking at his men, and can often be heard throughout the floor of the plant in which he works. Nonetheless, his men respect him. Although they keep their distance, they know that Mr. Hanson will see that they always meet their production schedules—and that he treats them all in the same manner. There is an element of fairness in yelling at *everybody* and subjecting all to the same treatment. Mr. Hanson is a good example of the *Chief* managerial style. He is a Producer and operates at the first level of managerial development.

---

father- or mother-figure. Their style becomes that of the *Patriarch* or *Matriarch*. They still insist on rules and procedures but recognize the need for making exceptions in individual circumstances. Individuals in need may not only be exempted from following standard procedures—for a time—but will also receive support and assistance in a time of crisis. The Patriarch/Matriarch still believes, however, in a logical, hierarchical universe, but one tempered by human understanding. As if the head of a large family, this Producer takes care of his or her own. (See Example 4.2.)

Example 4.2 Producers as Managers: Patriarchs

Tom Jacobs is a 32-year-old engineer in the testing division of a large industrial company. He is in charge of all the instruments used in testing and supervises a group of four other men. Although his superiors chide him for not seeing the "big picture," his men love him. He works closely with them, knows everything about instrumentation, and stands up for them in whatever situation occurs. He is warm and responsive to his men, but basically, believes that good management is being consistent, fair, and getting the work done. He is unhappy that his unit is not managed in the same way he runs his own group—and that all standards and procedures are not enforced on a regular basis. He believes that if his unit manager would take the time to enforce the regulations, everyone would be more effective—and more satisfied. Mr. Jacobs is a *Patriarch* in managerial style. His basic preference for rules and regulations has been supplemented by a genuine concern for "his people." He does not, however, step back and let them assume significant responsibility for themselves.

Growing into a larger arena, the Producer may next become a *Clan Leader*, delegating responsibilities to other members of the clan who have earned that responsibility. Less involved in the immediate doings of the work establishment, the Clan Leader recognizes his or her importance as a symbol to others. The Clan Leader upholds the rule of standards and procedures from afar and may even take time out to pursue his or her own individual interests. Clan Leaders at this stage of development often have developed their own particular hobbies or other pursuits, which do not compete with but complement the work experience. The distance thus created between the leader and the clan allows employees to take on more responsibility than with other managerial Producers.

With each level of development, the Producer achieves a greater balance. Initially most at home in pyramids, with maturity, Producers modify their styles so that pyramidal cones are their systems of preference. Still emphasizing procedures, still with a strong belief in hierarchy, Producers at higher levels have become participative managers, allowing those beneath them to assume greater responsibilities for both decision making and implementation of procedures. The Clan Leader has developed a degree of flexibility for managing in uncertain times. (See Figure 4.1.)

Processors as Managers

Processors begin at the other end of the continuum, with a set of expectations that emphasizes the importance of interpersonal interaction among individuals. As managers, they focus on the morale of their people. The young Processor, therefore, begins as a *Counselor*, working on a one-to-one basis with employees, encouraging them to work through their personal problems and devote themselves to their work. Available at almost all times, they invite their employees to visit them—and generally they do. However, when decisions need to be made quickly and action must be taken, the beginning Processor is at a disadvantage. Never having emphasized rules, procedures, or chains of command, the tools for rapid movement are rarely available. Decisions are made slowly by individuals working together—sometimes three steps behind everybody else. (See Example 4.3.)

FIGURE 4.1
MANAGEMENT STYLES I

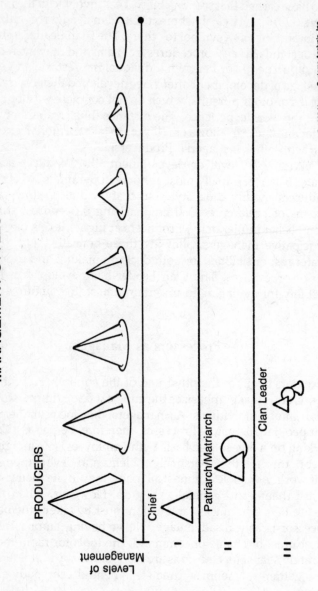

Example 4.3 Processors as Managers: Counselors

Jim Parkinson is the young assistant director of research for a new high technology company. He is charged with supervising much of the ongoing research of the firm and creating some of the procedures for detecting problems in new software packages. He can often be seen at his desk, feet propped up on the cluttered surface, smoking a cigarette and gazing out of the window. When he gets down to work, however, he works intently and feverishly and will stay at the office into the night in order to complete a project or develop a new idea.

Mr. Parkinson has two subordinates who monitor the debugging of new programs and actually carry out the work that tests his ideas. He is nonchalant, however, when asked about his own management and supervision style. "As long as they feel good about their work," he says, "I don't have to interfere much. One of them had some personal problems last week, and we spent several hours talking about them and working through his difficulties, and then we got back to work. I rarely do more than that." Mr. Parkinson's employees, however, much as they like him, often complain to each other than he neither gives clear enough directions nor tells them specifically what to do. Still, they feel very strongly about him and are willing to try and untangle any vague directions that come their way. Mr. Parkinson is a *Processor* in personality style and a *Counselor* in managerial style.

As Processors grow into higher levels of development, however, they accept the imperative of getting things done—and some of the inequalities that necessarily occur when the focus becomes task-oriented. The Processor takes a new view of the managerial role and becomes a *Facilitator*. At this level, the Processor not only counsels and coaches others but encourages and demands that they perform. Snags in performance schedules are still worked through on a one-to-one level, focusing on individual problems, but just as often they are worked through in dealing with an entire group. Still with a strong belief in the worth of the individual, the Facilitator sets the atmosphere in which people not only feel worthwhile but are encouraged to perform to the top of their abilities. (See Example 4.4.)

Only in full maturity does the Processor, basically focused on individuals, recognize the importance of systems. As the Processor moves into larger arenas, dealing with more and more groups, the interrelationship of all groups within larger organizational systems becomes a major part of the Processor's world view. At this point,

Example 4.4 Processors as Managers: Facilitators

Susan Clark is a 35-year-old manager in the marketing division of a major corporation. Recently, she has taken on some of the training responsibilities for the corporation. She is personally very interested in the human relations side of training, in communication, teamwork and decision making. She has been instrumental in bringing programs connected with these topics into the company. When she succeeds in doing this, she sits back, an interested observer, and takes satisfaction in having created an environment in which employees can learn and grow.

In setting up the seminars for training, however, she is said not to be as assertive as some other individuals. She believes that individuals should come to such sessions voluntarily and does little to insure that employees keep their initial commitments. Consequently, seminars set up by Ms. Clark are usually strong on supportiveness and openness, but a little "iffy" in terms of numbers of participants. Those who come benefit from the experience, but little is done to win over the recalcitrants. Ms. Clark is a *Facilitator* in management style, willing to create growth-producing environments—and to sit back and watch growth happen.

---

the Processor as manager becomes a skillful *Negotiator*, defining the rules and procedures by which groups interact. Rather than working with individuals alone, the Negotiator creates and monitors the systems by which groups of individuals can work with each other. Still working in the background in a supportive role, the Negotiator is able to manage the complexities of large systems by developing the rules for the subsystems to work with each other.

Each step of development achieves a greater balance for the Processor. Originating at the other end of the management continuum than the Producer, the Processor as manager changes his or her preference for the circular structure to that of the circular cone. Still relatively flat, the development of the cone reflects the ability of highly developed Processors to get things done as well as to talk about it, to emphasize achievement and to standardize some rules as well as to focus on employee morale. The Negotiator has developed sufficient flexibility to manage a large system effectively and productively. (See Figure 4.2.)

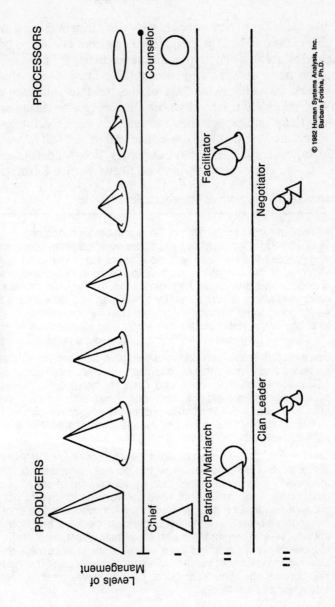

FIGURE 4.2
MANAGEMENT STYLES II

© 1982 Human Systems Analysis, Inc.
Barbara Forisha, Ph.D.

Integrators as Managers

Unlike the other two personality styles, the Integrator as a manager begins in the middle. The Integrator starts from a balanced position, with an awareness of both pyramids and circles, the need to achieve and the need to work with others. The Integrator at this level, however, has little awareness of the need to influence others. Rather, relatively balanced within, the Integrator leaves management to itself and expects to run a system by example. Integrators at this level are *Role Models*. They will lead if others will follow, doing little, however, to insure that this occurs. Role Models take care of themselves and expect others to do likewise. (See Example 4.5.)

Example 4.5 Integrators as Managers: Role Models

Aileen Danton is the manager of the newsroom for a local radio station. She has been in the job for ten years. Her work has always been superb and she has tied up more and more of her life in her job. Recently, changes at the top of the national corporation necessitated some changes in supervision at the radio station. The general manager, an easygoing fellow, was replaced by a new man who felt insecure in his position and began tightening the rules. The new general manager then took one of the staff from the newsroom and elevated him to project director—and, therefore, Ms. Danton's immediate supervisor.

The project director, Tony Bartholomew, gave little credit to Ms. Danton, for he wanted to make this *his* operation. He discounted her work and asked her instead what she had done for her people. He wanted accountings of time, projects, and accomplishments for the last year. Ms. Danton had led her unit in the past by focusing on her own work and by being best at what she did. Her subordinates learned to do their own work by watching and modeling her.

Ms. Danton had successfully used the style of *Role Model* until the arrival of Tony Bartholomew. Now, her job was in jeopardy for she had managed by example, rather than by supervision of schedules and procedures, and she did not have the records to give to her new supervisor. Although her unit turned toward collecting this data, Ms. Danton was bitter and unhappy. In the past, her work had been most important—and her staff had worked, without direct supervision, right along with her. To shift her focus to their work, to encourage them to achieve and to limit her own achievement, were not part of her managerial expectations. She was still at the first developmental level, an Integrator as Role Model.

At the next level of development, however, Integrators realize that all people are not alike, that setting examples is insufficient, and that it is necessary to assume some responsibility for the awareness of others. At this stage, Integrators become *Team Leaders*, using their influence to move others toward common goals. Changing the primary pronoun from "I" to "we," Integrators now work with others to encourage them to achieve. Less focused on individual achievement (what *I* can do), Integrators become effective as group leaders and focus on group achievement (what *we* can do). Establishing procedures and showing support, effective Team Leaders move their groups down the field to the final goal. (See Example 4.6.)

Example 4.6 Integrators as Managers: Team Leaders

Paul Edwards is about to be promoted to principal engineer, manager of seven other engineers. He has worked successfully in a lesser position, primarily alone, for the last four years. His ability to get his work done effectively and to get along with his boss and the current principal engineer have led to his imminent promotion. Mr. Edwards is one of the few men in the unit who is able to recognize the talents of other individuals at the same time as he understands the constraints of the system. He has a good deal of "organizational sense" as well as technical competence. In the last four years, however, his efforts have focused on making his own work excellent. His boss is worried that he may not understand fully that he cannot manage by example, but instead must recognize where his subordinates are, perceive and use their idiosyncratic strengths, and respect their limitations. Mr. Edwards is, however, beginning to see that he must enlarge his picture of management as he moves into a role. He sees, in forecasting the future, that he will operate as a Team Leader, recognizing and using the individual strengths of his men. It is still hard for him at this point, however, to focus his attention on helping others to achieve rather than achieving himself.

At even higher levels, however, Integrators learn to be *Systems Coordinators*, creating the rules and procedures that will help many groups achieve their own goals within the boundaries of the larger system. Intent on building a functioning system, the Systems Coordinator will establish the procedures that allow all units to function well. Taking less of an up-front position than the Producer, and less of a back seat than the Processor, the Systems Coordinator stands in between, building the master plan that will let each group work productively and satisfactorily.

The Integrator begins with a modicum of balance, poised in between the two ends of the continuum. Yet, this Integrator, like other beginners, still has a narrower vision than is necessary for full effectiveness. The balance reflected by the early Integrator is an inner balance, focused on self. With experience and maturity, the Integrator learns first to acknowledge systems and then group differences and to develop a balance that includes not just self but others—and the larger world. The experienced Systems Coordinator has achieved a new level of balance, encompassing larger and larger arenas, that brings much more perspective to his or her managerial view than that of the beginning Integrator. The system of preference for the Systems Coordinator is thus nearly centered on the continuum but leans slightly toward the end of letting others do for themselves what they can best do. (See Figure 4.3.)

Management and Personality Styles

Effective management makes the best use of both material and human resources, thus achieving maximum output from minimum input. In order to do this in times of uncertainty, communication lines must be open, decision-making structures must be established, and people at the top must have the good judgment to choose the most likely course for achieving both productivity and satisfaction. The people at the top exhibit all personality styles, depending on the nature of the unit and the organization. Although Integrators predominate in these positions, Producers and Processors find themselves there as well. It is imperative that these individuals all be able to recognize the joint importance of the individual and the system and harness these resources to achieve organizational goals. This can happen only when a balance between human needs and task priorities is established, when individuals are open to new alternatives for action and capable of selecting the most appropriate one.

All managers at lower levels of development have difficulty doing this, as each is focused on only a limited area of the management spectrum. Early Producers see procedures, Integrators see personal achievement, and Processors see employee morale. How-

FIGURE 4.3
MANAGEMENT STYLES III

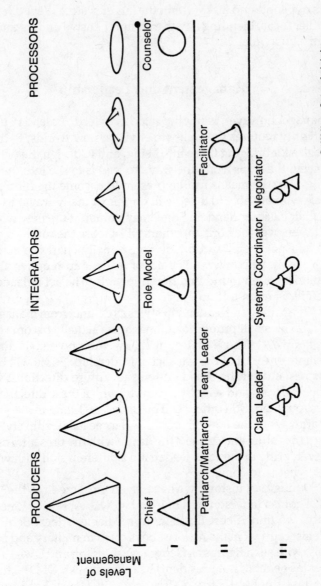

PRODUCERS   INTEGRATORS   PROCESSORS

Levels of Management

I   Chief   Role Model   Counselor

II   Patriarch/Matriarch   Team Leader   Facilitator

III   Clan Leader   Systems Coordinator   Negotiator

ever, as each style progresses in experience and maturity, each develops a greater breadth of vision. Each is able to integrate the needs of people and tasks within the larger system. Yet each retains its earlier focus, blending it with a comprehensive understanding of organizational life.

Management and Leadership

To manage, however, is not the same as to lead. To lead in times of uncertainty requires the ability to envision new worlds, to develop strategies for bringing those into being, and to design the plans that will detail the steps along the way. To lead is to see into the future and develop the means for the present to become the future. Individuals who are able to do so will do this in many ways, in accord with their basic tendencies. Some may point out the new worlds as yet unseen over the horizon, others will choose the course by which we might get there, and others will actually chart the course by which we make our way. The act of leadership requires all three capabilities, often found in different people. The act of leadership, therefore, is often a team effort.

We are defining leadership styles as distinct from management styles. Some small proportion of managers actually become leaders (see Figure 4.4). Those that do will have their own style and each contribute one part of the total act of leadership. Some will become *Visionaries* and set the broad outlines for future directions. Others will be *Strategists* and select the paths by which these directions may be best pursued. Still others will be *Designers*, filling in step by step the pathways of the new directions. All three leadership styles look toward the future and connect the future with the present. All three, however, bring to the act of leadership a different skill with which to shape what is to come.

Throughout history, we have given most credit to the Visionaries. Thomas Jefferson was one and so was Abraham Lincoln. In science, we find Albert Einstein; in medicine, Albert Schweitzer. Strategists appear in the history books often in military and political realms, with such figures as George Washington and Dwight Eisenhower (as general, not president) heading the list. Of Designers we know less, though Harry S. Truman and Henry Ford are good candidates for this leadership style, blended with a bit of the Strat-

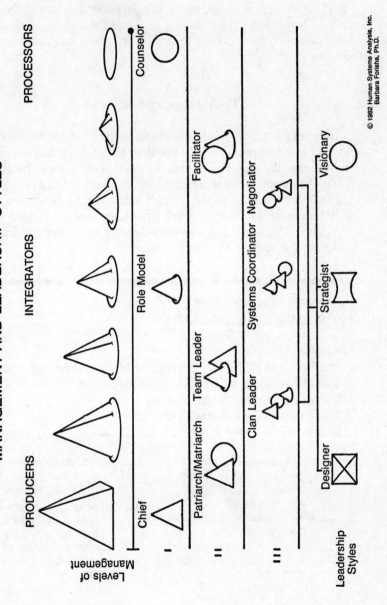

FIGURE 4.4
MANAGEMENT AND LEADERSHIP STYLES

© 1982 Human Systems Analysis, Inc.
Barbara Forisha, Ph.D.

PRODUCERS   INTEGRATORS   PROCESSORS

Levels of Management

Chief   Patriarch/Matriarch   Team Leader   Role Model   Facilitator   Counselor

Clan Leader   Systems Coordinator   Negotiator

Designer   Strategist   Visionary

Leadership Styles

egist. Yet every Designer follows in the steps of Strategists and Visionaries who have outlined new directions, and every Visionary stands in front of a number of Strategists and Designers who were able to implement the outlines of a new world. In each act of leadership, all three styles are essential. Each contributes to the whole.

To Manage and to Lead

In times of uncertainty, all individuals with the ability to work with others have a responsibility to use their talents both to manage and to lead, to take care of the present even as they look toward the future. They may do so in informal or formal ways, from positions of minimal authority to those of high authority. In each case, such individuals will be most effective when they seek a balanced vision of what is and what can be—and develop the inner flexibility to adapt and shape the forces of change.

EXERCISE: MINI-ORGANIZATIONAL
PROBLEM-SOLVING INVENTORY

Instructions:
In the box next to each statement, write a number from 1 to 4.
    4—I almost always agree with this statement.
    3—I often agree with this statement.
    2—I occasionally agree with this statement.
    1—I rarely or never agree with this statement.

_____ ☐ The causes of most problems can be clearly isolated and defined in concrete terms.

_____ ■ Even small changes may have great effects.

_____ ☐ The worth of any project can be measured in dollars and cents.

_____ ☐ Good projects involve low risk to individuals and short-term rewards.

_____ ■ Sometimes strange or unusual solutions to problems may have a better probability of success than standard practices.

_____ ☐ The best way to resolve problems will minimize risk to all involved.

_____ ☐ Worthwhile solutions to problems will necessarily have visible and positive short-run consequences.

_____ ☐ Each step of an action plan must be completed on schedule for the project to be successful.

_____ ☐ Most problems can be explained in simple, easily understood language.

_____ ☐ Major organizational problems can generally be resolved by increasing or improving technological resources.

_____ ■ Sometimes the best solutions to problems require high commitments of time and energy from everybody involved.

_____ ☐ Any project that can actually be completed is significant.

_____ ☐ The value of any project should be self-evident, so that little time is wasted persuading others of its worth.

_____ ■ Action plans must be flexible to account for unpredictable happenings in human lives.

_____ ☐ Work teams made up of ordinary people cannot expect extraordinary results.

_____ ☐ A good solution easily wins the approval of those involved.

_____ ☐ Outcomes that cannot be easily measured have no place in action plans.

_____ ■ Problems can often be best stated in terms of parables or other symbolic communication.

_____ ■ The best solution may be arrived at as a result of insight rather than logic.

_____ ☐ Individuals will invest time and energy only in projects that offer them tangible rewards.

_____ ■ Some worthwhile projects require more personal risk with less likelihood of personal gain.

_____ ☐ Problems that occurred in the past have little to do with what is happening now.

_____ ☐ Considering more than three alternative solutions to a problem is generally a waste of time.

_____ ■ A problem is often only a symptom of a more serious underlying difficulty in human relationships.

Scoring:
To find your problem-solving (leadership) style, first add up all the numbers in the plain boxes. Then add up all the numbers in the

shaded boxes. Subtract the plain box sum from the shaded box sum and divide your answer by 2.

You are probably a Designer if you scored less than −2.

You are probably a Visionary if you scored more than +2.

You are probably a Strategist if you scored between −2 and +2.

5

Effective Work Groups in Pyramids and Circles

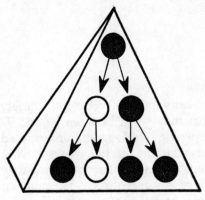

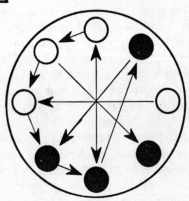

A group of manufacturing supervisors and managers from a variety of plants recently estimated that they spent between 90 and 99 percent of their time with other people. The longest uninterrupted period of time they had experienced in the last two weeks at work was one hour, but the average amount of uninterrupted time they experienced for the last two weeks was between five and ten minutes. This group of managers is typical of managers and supervisors in general. Most managerial time is spent in the company of others, either in groups, on a one-to-one basis, or on the telephone. Most managerial time is spent talking or listening to others. Little time is spent alone or in independent activity.

Despite the fact that management is a group activity, much of our thinking about managers and management has focused on the individual. Americans have a cultural history that focuses on the individual, not the group, and as a consequence we have perceived the organizational landscape peopled by individuals, sometimes in isolation from each other. A truer picture would be to view the landscape dotted with many groups of interconnected individuals. Our belief in independence has caused us to slight the real interdependence of each individual with the group—and with the larger system composed of many groups.

In this time of transition, however, as corporations reevaluate themselves, they are highlighting the importance of individuals working together rather than alone. They are realizing that management is a group activity and that the ability to work well with others is the key to managerial effectiveness. As individuals in corporations are becoming more aware of the importance of group activity, each is asking the obvious questions: Given that I spend most of my time with others, how do I make this time productive? If I am going to spend even more of my life in company with others, how do I make this time count? The increased awareness of the centrality of group activity in organizations has appropriately focused attention on the ineffectiveness of many group encounters. The effectiveness of group activity is one of the most important factors in improving use of our human resources—and, hence, increasing our productivity. Stretching a bit, one might suggest that the viability of group interaction is at the root of organizational survival.

Groups as Pyramids and Circles

Any group of individuals together for any length of time begins to take on a shape of its own, determined by the patterns of human interaction that become established within the group. The shapes established by the patterns of interaction may be described as relatively pyramidal or circular. Just as larger organizations tend to develop a hierarchy or lie flat against the ground, so do all smaller groups. Thus, effective groups will either have a recognized leader who respects and accepts all group members, or they will be primarily leaderless, with each member performing a relatively equal and valued function within the group. Most groups do not assume, however, these absolute forms. Rather, pyramidal groups have an identifiable leader who sometimes interacts on a peer level with other members of the group, and circular groups often have a leader for a time who takes responsibility for the decisions and actions of the group. Still, groups may be identified as primarily pyramidal or circular.

Ineffective groups are similar to crooked pyramids and squishy circles. Within a small group as well as a large one, one member may dominate others, creating resentment, hostility, and/or apathy among group members. Also, small groups, nominally without a leader, may cling together to repel outside forces, limiting their own autonomy and their openness to new information. The boss as tyrant is a symbol of the crooked pyramid. The interminable, do-nothing meeting is a symbol of the squishy circle. With a new awareness of the importance of group activity in organizations, it is imperative that we learn to discriminate effective and ineffective groups from each other and learn to turn the latter into the former. In learning to work together in organizations, we move one step closer to economic survival and productivity.

The Small Group as Pyramid

Pyramidal work groups are often composed of natural work teams that include a boss and several subordinates, or they are brought together as a specific task force to focus on one issue. Pyramidal groups are designed to get things done and to accomplish specific tasks. They are designed as mini-hierarchies with a leader and several followers, although the followers may vary in rank, some assuming various degrees of leadership themselves. Psychologically, effective pyramidal work groups result in higher self-esteem for each member, based on a sense of accomplishment. In terms of structure, effective pyramids occur most often when the formal leader of the group (according to the organizational chart) also has the informal power to actually lead the group.

As we think about groups, we tend to see them operating in an either-or fashion. Either the pyramidal group is functioning smoothly, with directions flowing downward, respect beaming upward, and work output the result (see Figure 5.1), or we view the mini-pyramid as a scene of tension and resentment with crises provoking an uneven work flow (see Figure 5.2). We imagine the ideal, a harmonious group, with everybody having the same understanding of functions and goals, or we perceive the worst, a stress-ridden group in which each person aggrandizes himself or herself at the expense of another. Instead, we might find the reality—and the basis for effectiveness—in between.

FIGURE 5.1
THE IDEA OF A PYRAMIDAL TEAM

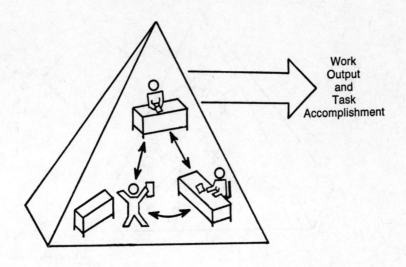

Work Output and Task Accomplishment

A set of expectations that leads to productivity in pyramidal groups recognizes individual differences. The ways in which the boss operates may be different from those of subordinates, and each subordinate may be different from the other. The boss may be a Producer, a rules-and-procedures woman, and the subordinate may be an Integrator, interested in running the show. Or the boss may be a Processor, a man focused on morale and individual satisfaction, and the subordinate may be a Producer, wanting to know what to do and when to do it rather than focusing on interpersonal interaction. In each case, an awareness of one's own style and that of others may help individuals work together productively.

Realistic expectations of situational differences also further a productive and effective work effort by a pyramidal group. Some situations require rapid action—and often a decision by the boss in order to meet time deadlines and to focus productivity of the entire

FIGURE 5.2
THE REALITY OF A PYRAMIDAL TEAM

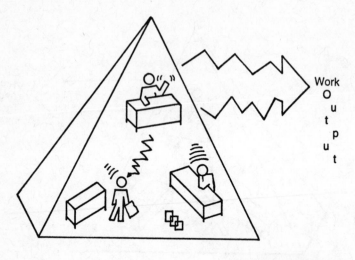

Work
O
u
t
p
u
t

team. Some situations require decisions made over time, so that ultimate decisions will be based on as much information as possible. Individuals adapt to both situations more easily when they expect that both will occur—and that neither is the forced creation of another individual but a result of living in a changing environment.

Within pyramids then, individuals are effective when they adapt to both individual and situational differences. As they do so, the division of work within the team may be realigned to meet individual strengths and the demands of the environment. Exact job descriptions may be altered alightly in order to give individuals the work assignments most suited to their talents. The rules-and-procedures boss may recognize the need for some responsibility on the part of her subordinates and allow them to manage specific projects while she maintains the schedules and the procedural uniformity. The manager focused on morale may spend time coaching employees and encouraging others in the group to formulate the rules, procedures, and timetables for task accomplishment. In a sense, each work group is unique, and work patterns that are tailored to each particular group increase effectiveness.

To summarize, the idea of a work group, composed of similar individuals in a stable environment, may diminish productivity by increasing resentment that things are not the way they are supposed to be. The reality of a work group, once acknowledged, however, can become the basis for an effective unit. Two illustrations of work groups struggling to become effective, upright pyramids are given in Examples 5.1 and 5.2.

Example 5.1 Straightening up a Pyramidal Group

When the formal and informal power is centered on the technical head of a unit, it is likely that this group will function primarily as a pyramid. There is a vast difference, however, between effective and ineffective pyramids.

In one supervisory unit, the formal and informal power was centered on the general supervisor, who then oversaw the work of three shift supervisors. The general supervisor was a competent, thoughtful man who nonetheless held himself and his unit to very high expectations. As a consequence of expecting so much, he was often disappointed and frustrated, but he accepted this wryly as part of life. His three shift supervisors varied in ability: one was very good with people but a little too easygoing; another was a grumpy, white-haired man who "chewed out" the men frequently but did know what he was doing technically; and the third was largely incompetent but covered for by the other two.

The unit was a moderately effective pyramid. If the general supervisor held to his expectations and took his frustrations out on his men, the unit would become ineffective, and the shift supervisors would coalesce against the boss. The unit would then be described as a crooked pyramid. On the other hand, if the general supervisor were perceived as more open by his subordinates, they might confide in him the difficulties they perceived with the incompetent third supervisor. Once the problem was in the open, they might all do something to improve this supervisor's competence or to lessen his work load—or to work through whatever personal problems were hindering his performance.

At this time, they have been confronted with the discrepancies in abilities between the shift supervisors, and the group as a whole is committed to working out a better balance of expectations and abilities. Whether or not the unit may become an upright pyramid is still to be seen.

Example 5.2 Changing Circles into Pyramids

In another case, the top management team of a manufacturing unit could best be described as a squishy circle. The boss, Gerald Black, a warm, friendly man who likes to talk with his men, was vague in his directions to them and often called them down for not doing what he expected—which he had never clearly communicated in the first place. Next in command was John Fallaway, an idealistic, unambitious thinker. His main charge was the day-to-day supervision of the unit. He paid so little attention, in general, to the day-to-day activities that his supervision was haphazard and perceived as inconsistent and uncaring. He was accused of playing favorites and playing politics. The two men at the next level were both more powerful than Mr. Fallaway. Carl Thomas was a forthright, sturdy man who believed in more work and less talk, and withdrew from the discussions of the management team to attend to his day-to-day business. Finally, Martin Moore, already picked to move upward the fastest, was a competent, intelligent, and warm person but overly aggressive in his contacts with others. Martin continually tried to move the unit in a positive (according to him) direction and resorted to bulldozing his way through when agreement was not forthcoming. His lower status prevented him from being successful in his efforts to get his way by authoritative statements. Power in this unit, centered at the bottom, shared by both Mr. Thomas and particularly Mr. Moore, labeled the unit a circle. The ineffectiveness of either man in persuading the unit to move in directions they believed appropriate led to Mr. Thomas's withdrawal and Mr. Moore's aggression.

A change in the formal structure, which, with the concurrence of Mr. Thomas, increased Mr. Moore's status and removed Mr. Fallaway from the supervisory scene, has created an effective pyramid with Mr. Moore in charge. His opinions are now adhered to by the others. The boss, Mr. Black, is now free to talk and generate ideas with his men, knowing that the unit is being run effectively by his immediate subordinate.

The Small Group as Circle

Circular work groups often develop from peer groups, sometimes for overtly social purposes, or they may be brought together as committees or problem-solving groups. The most common setting for the circle is the conference room of the organization. Circular groups are designed to share information and generate ideas to problem situations. They are flat in nature, assuming equality among members—at least in this particular setting. Psychologically, effective circular work groups will result in increased self-esteem, based on a sense of belonging and involvement in the decision-making process.

Just as with pyramidal groups, circular groups are often viewed in an either-or fashion. We commonly have an *idea* that all members of a circular group share a similar purpose, are well prepared for a meeting, and are interested in and attentive to the group process. We reveal our belief in this idea whenever we complain that so-and-so is not doing his or her share. Group members' complaints about each other are a continuous part of much group functioning and suggest that members expect that circular groups (committee meetings, discussion groups, and so forth) will generate an uninterrupted series of ideas and alternatives for solving problems (see Figure 5.3). When this idea proves false, and members do not

FIGURE 5.3
THE IDEA OF A CIRCULAR TEAM

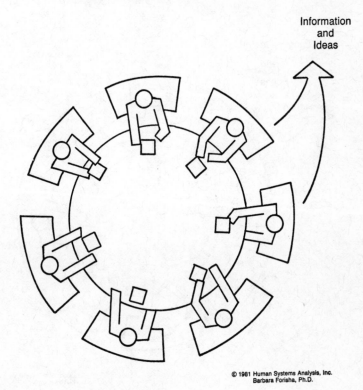

Information
and
Ideas

contribute relatively equally to this process, we often perceive quite a different scenario in which some people run the show and others retreat in apathy or resentment (see Figure 5.4).

The reality lies in between. With the acceptance that different individuals make different contributions, we have the basis for developing an effective circular group. Informally, the group may draw upon the various individual strengths. Producers, for example, may be relied upon for monitoring procedures, and Processors for their social ease and occasional insight. Integrators may provide the structure that holds the group together and focuses attention on the goals and purposes of the unit.

In circular as in pyramidal groups, the shape of the group must

FIGURE 5.4
THE REALITY OF A CIRCULAR TEAM

Information
and
Ideas

also adapt to situational as well as individual differences. Occasionally the group may have no pressing concerns and be relaxed and sociable. At other times, urgent matters may either distract the attention of some members or focus them intensely on the subject matter under discussion. A recognition of variations in situation just as in personality styles is essential for effective group functioning. Illustrations of work groups operating—finally—as effective circles are given in Examples 5.3 and 5.4.

Example 5.3 Creating an Effective Circle

Some groups function more effectively as circles and some as pyramids. In one supervisory unit (in the same company as that described in Example 5.1), a group of three shift supervisors and a general supervisor were functioning ineffectively—rather like a squishy circle. The three shift supervisors had all been there quite a long time, longer than their superior. They were all relatively powerful and respected by their men. One among them was regarded as an expert in human relations, another an expert in technical areas, the third was generally the mediator when debates arose. The general supervisor had entered this unit when the shift supervisors had been functioning together over three or four years. The general supervisor expected to assume command of the unit and to issue orders. His orders were generally ignored and the team of three shift supervisors continued to run the show. The squishiness of their circle came from the fact that informally they deliberately—and with some effort—managed to exclude their boss from any decision-making function.

A diagnosis of the unit showed that it was unlikely that this group would turn themselves into an effective pyramid—in which the boss assumes both formal and informal power and others follow his lead. Rather, this unit, with more openness toward the boss, might turn itself into an effective circle in which all shared in the decision-making process on an informal level. Several months of training followed and the unit *did* become an effective circle. The boss relinquished his hope of supreme power and agreed to join his men on a semi-peer-level relationship. The team of three benefited from acknowledging the input of the boss, for although they shared much competence among them, none had the ability to be clear and decisive in setting their expectations of themselves and each other. The willingness of the shift supervisors to recognize their boss informally meant that a decisive voice was added to their pool of team talents, which already included skills in human relations, mediation and technical areas. The improved effectiveness of all supervisors was documented in the evaluations of this supervisory team by their subordinates. They now operate as an effective circle.

Example 5.4 Changing Pyramids into Circles

During a seminar in management development, one work group's behavior moved from a crooked pyramid to a round circle. In initial
problem-solving sessions, George Paxton, the plant manager, dominated conversation. The superintendent and assistant superintendent,
both competent and able men, hunched over in their chairs and ac-
ceded to the direction set by Mr. Paxton. The superintendent later said
that he was so seething with resentment that he was afraid to open his
mouth for fear of what might come out. The assistant superintendent
said he was often either silent or angry in such a setting and silence
seemed the better alternative. The plant manager, Mr. Paxton, was
totally unaware of their feelings and assumed the discussion and decision had been the choice of the entire group. . . .

Two days later, after extensive discussion of his behavior, aided by
videotape feedback, Mr. Paxton was able to turn his strength from
domination to responsive guidance of the group process. Biting his lip at
times to keep from leaping into the fray with his own opinions, he
created an atmosphere in which all members of the group offered and
discussed opinions. The superintendent emerged as a strong, responsive leader able to side with the plant manager. The assistant superintendent offered his opinions without anger but with firmness. Other
members of the group said it was the best discussion that they had ever
had with their work team. In exercising great restraint, plant management discovered new alliances and new strengths among themselves.
The personal power used to dominate and create a crooked pyramid
had been channeled into firmness and responsiveness, and the result
was an effective circle.

Alternating Pyramids and Circles

Most individuals in organizations operate in both pyramidal and
circular groups—and improve their own effectiveness when they
can demonstrate the behaviors that are appropriate to the immediate group. A task-centered orientation and acceptance of a
hierarchical chain of command is appropriate for the pyramidal
setting. A people-centered orientation and responsiveness to the
ideas of all members is appropriate for a circular setting. To the
degree that individuals develop a repertoire of behaviors appropriate for both settings, they increase their own flexibility and effectiveness in the face of changing circumstances.

Groups too, whether pyramidal or circular, increase their effectiveness by maintaining their flexibility. The shape of the group may change to meet the requirements of conditions existing both inside and outside the group. Formal or informal roles may be designed to make the most of individual strengths. The pyramidal or circular nature of the group may shift to meet demands for task accomplishment or problem solving. Groups that fail to maintain this flexibility become rigid and impermeable over time. Pyramids that fail to become circles from time to time will remain closed to new ideas, and circles that fail to become pyramids once in a while will lose the opportunity to implement ideas. In a structural sense, then, as in the individual sense, the key to effectiveness is flexibility.

Effective groups, therefore, are flexible in assigning roles to group members and in adopting the overall structure most suited to the situation at hand. As we turn now to the process that occurs in groups, we will shift our focus from styles and structures to the impact of communication and expectations within and among groups. The interaction that makes a group a group is the communication among individuals. The foundation for much of this communication rests on the expectations of group members, subsumed under the headings of group traditions, group customs, and group norms. Both communication and group norms will be examined in the following chapters. When communication is clear and group norms are constructive, most work groups operate effectively as upright pyramids and round circles—with structures alternating to best fit the individuals and the situation.

EXERCISE: MINI-GROUP PERCEPTIONS INVENTORY

Instructions:

In the box next to each statement, write a number from 1 to 4. According to my perceptions of my work group, they are:

4—almost always this way
3—often this way
2—occasionally this way
1—rarely or never this way

_____ □ Unwilling to share personal experiences with others

_____ ■ Interested in discovering the patterns reflected in different viewpoints

71

_____ ☐ Careful to leave before an argument begins

_____ ☐ Uneasy with any decision that upsets people

_____ ■ Unwilling to see any matter as completely closed

_____ ☐ Not likely to be aware of current trends

_____ ☐ Reluctant to identify with common goals

_____ ☐ Likely to make the same decision over and over again

_____ ☐ Certain that luck is a critical factor in achieving anything

_____ ☐ Willing to let other people take care of the details

_____ ■ Open to alternative ways of accomplishing tasks

_____ ☐ Likely to take rumors about us seriously

_____ ☐ Reluctant to make changes in daily routines

_____ ☐ Careful to keep one step ahead of other people

_____ ■ Reluctant to make final judgments on surface impressions

_____ ☐ Continually seeking approval and agreement

_____ ☐ Willing to give up when there are no immediate rewards

_____ ■ Open to sharing group rewards with all individuals

_____ ☐ Not interested in why people believe as they do

_____ ☐ Most concerned about how things _ought_ to be done

_____ ☐ Convinced that success has little to do with individual effort

_____ ■ Of the opinion that even good decisions need to be reevaluated in time

_____ ■ Willing to recognize and appreciate individual differences

_____ ☐ Convinced that once a project is begun the direction cannot be changed

_____ ☐ Opposed to seeing another person's viewpoint

_____ ☐ Reluctant to change something that already works

_____ ☐ Likely to avoid dealing with specific issues

_____ ■ Likely to direct conflict toward achieving a creative solution

_____ ☐ Confused about the differences between opinions and facts

_____ ☐ Reluctant to arrive at any decision of consequence

_____ ■ Likely to consider the feelings of others in most situations

_____ ■ Supportive of other individuals in the face of setbacks

_____ ☐ Convinced that one person's success is paid for by others

_____ ☐ Given to making snap judgments about others

_____ ■ Able to change old beliefs to fit current experiences

_____ ■ Open to appreciating people for their unique qualities

Scoring:

To identify the personality style of your work group, first add up all the numbers in the plain boxes. Then add up all the numbers in the shaded boxes. Subtract the plain box sum from the shaded box sum and divide your answer by 3.

Your group is probably made up largely of Producers who operate best in Pyramids if your score is less than -2.

Your group is probably made up largely of Processors who operate best in Circles if your score is more than $+2$.

Your group is probably made up largely of Integrators who operate best in Cones if your score is between -2 and $+2$.

6

Communication
and Group Effectiveness
in Pyramids and Circles

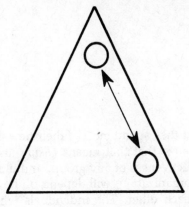

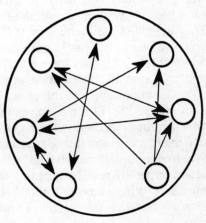

Managers, in acknowledging that they spend most of their time in company with other people, realize that that means *talking* and *listening* to other people. The effectiveness of any group, and ultimately the effectiveness of any organization, will depend on how well people talk and listen to each other. The individuals who communicate well often become the leaders of the organization. They are able to tell others what they think and also listen to the opinions of others. They know what they think and they learn what others think. Thus they learn about themselves and their organization and gather the information on which to base effective decisions.

Communication is, therefore, the fundamental process in organizational life. Effective communication is the process through which groups knit themselves together, and ineffective communication may unravel any threads that connect one person with another. When communication between individuals is effective, group interaction generally results in productivity and satisfaction for group members. When communication between individuals is ineffective, group interaction may result in lowered productivity and satisfaction.

Any group's progress toward effective interaction may be

measured by observing the verbal and nonverbal communication of individual members. As individuals talk, move, gesture, turn away, or lean forward, they tell each other what they think of themselves and the group. As they work together over time they shape themselves into mini-pyramids or mini-circles and in turn are influenced by the expectations that accompany each particular structure. The nature of their communication in both pyramids and circles will either create or destroy the connections that are the essence of an effective group.

Shared Expectations

The effectiveness of the group depends upon the connections that group members develop among themselves. The strength of the connections rests upon the degree to which members have acknowledged a set of shared expectations common to all group members. When the shared expectations mesh with the stated purposes of a group, they form the basis for productive and satisfying interaction. Group members expect to do what they say they will. When this cohesion is present, disparate expectations of some individual members may enliven group interaction without destroying it. When shared expectations, however, do not mesh with the stated purposes of the group but instead focus, however unconsciously, on avoiding accomplishing the stated purposes, the group as currently constituted may disband in order to pursue other goals (see Figure 6.1).

The process of uncovering shared expectations involves the willingness of each group member to share personal expectations and to listen to those of others. As individuals share their own expectations with each other, they test and challenge each other. As they find that others share some of their own views of people and the world, they grow in acceptance of each other. This acceptance then is the foundation for effective group interaction. In an effective group where interaction is based on clear expectations there are no overwhelming surprises. All of the terrain on which they are operating is clearly lit, and individuals may circumvent pitfalls and walk confidently in the open spaces.

Groups that fail to uncover shared sets of expectations are subject to many hazards. Some group members, wary of unex-

FIGURE 6.1
SHARED EXPECTATIONS IN A GROUP

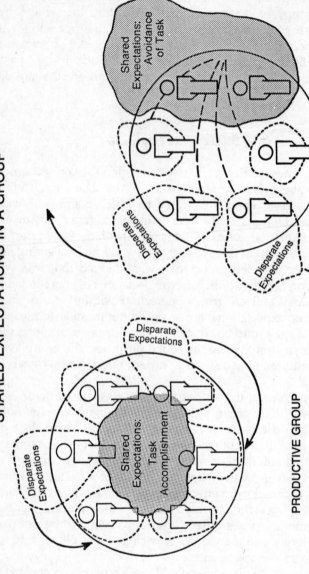

pected disagreement, may choose to be quiet and withdraw. Others may plunge forward, determined to sweep away all potential disagreements. Still others, unaware that their peers may think differently from themselves, will blithely express their own opinions and then be shocked and dismayed at the ensuing unexpected conflict. Operating without a common foundation, individuals in groups leave much to chance, resulting in generally lowered productivity and satisfaction.

Effective Communication

Creating a shared set of expectations requires that group members tell others what they think and listen as others tell them their own views. Telling others what one thinks is termed *directness* in communication. Listening to what others think is termed *responsiveness*. Communication that is both direct and responsive is effective. Through effective communication, group members forge lasting links with each other.

Very direct and very responsive. The importance of directness and responsiveness in communication cannot be overstated. Over a period of time we have watched individuals interacting in various groups and have concluded that individuals who are both very direct and responsive assume the roles of informal leaders within any group. As they state their own views, and listen to those of others, they guide the group in problem solving and decision making. The outcome of group process will clearly reflect the activities of the best communicators within that group setting. We have come to call these individuals *centers of influence* who are high in *change capability*. Such people not only achieve their own goals but help others achieve theirs.

Further, such individuals within groups who are both direct and responsive tend to develop these qualities in others. Over a period of time they do not stand head and shoulders above others but instead shoulder to shoulder with their peers. Such individuals, by not only stating their position but encouraging others to share theirs, elicit strength and develop talent in others. Consequently, over time, effective groups contain members who are direct and responsive, who are able to share their views and encourage others to do the same. The process of developing such an effective group, however, may begin with one person who is strong in both directness and responsiveness. Descriptions of two such individuals appear in Examples 6.1 and 6.2.

Example 6.1 Direct and Responsive Communication: Susan Tetweiler

Susan Tetweiler is a 55-year-old manager in a large service organization. She is highly regarded by those who work with her—as one coworker said, "Everybody just loves Susan." Her behavior in a committee meeting in which she won her point demonstrates why people both respect and love her. She was very clear about her own needs but also very warm and receptive to the ideas of others.

She began her presentation by looking around at the other members and saying, "I need your help." She went on to explain how she had no place to meet with her clients since another manager was using the only spare room in the building to store old equipment. She had asked him to move and he had removed materials from one shelf so that she would have a place for *her* materials, but he had not vacated the room. Committee members asked numerous questions about the allocation of space and the priority of various sorts of needs within the company. It looked for a minute as if Ms. Tetweiler might get swept away by their questions and give up her point. However, she sat up straighter, put her feet squarely on the floor, looked them all in the eye in turn, and said, "But you have to understand, I *want* that room." Immediately, the entire committee relaxed and laughed and said they would act to get it for her. The meeting concluded when one man joked, "Let's just simplify the process and put out a contract on him." They all left laughing, and Ms. Tetweiler now has her desired space.

Very direct and unresponsive. Many of our stereotypes of aggressive businessmen portray individuals who are very direct and unresponsive. The stereotypes also suggest that these individuals are highly successful within organizations. Our experience, on the other hand, has shown that this is not so. Rather, individuals who are aggressive (direct and unresponsive) are often highly visible within groups and within larger organizational units but they carry very little influence in problem solving and decision making. Such individuals are sometimes best characterized as *noisemakers,* rather like fireworks on the Fourth of July—except that their explosions are greeted with rather less satisfaction than genuine fireworks displays. Two groups whose meetings were characterized more by directness than responsiveness are described in Example 6.3.

Example 6.2 Direct and Responsive Communication: Kenneth Bachman

---

Kenneth Bachman is a 52-year-old manager in a major corporation. In a series of meetings of a task force, he demonstrated his ability to bring a group to consensus without forcefully taking the lead in the discussion. In early meetings of the task force, a conflict had developed between two other members: Bill Allerton, a forceful young man, designated as a brilliant comer in the organization, and Cal Dudley, a slightly older man who had a reputation for getting things done in the traditional manner. At the beginning of the task force meetings, Mr. Allerton and Mr. Dudley had locked horns on several issues. Mr. Allerton would present his point; Mr. Dudley would challenge it. Mr. Allerton would press his point, and Mr. Dudley would become angry. The first meeting ended with Mr. Allerton pounding the table, and Mr. Dudley sitting back in the chair scowling with his arms crossed and his eyes looking at the papers on the table.

During this initial session, Mr. Bachman occasionally made a point but spent most of the time watching and listening to the two other men. In later sessions, however, he moved his chair in closer and took a greater part in the discussion. He would often lean forward and state an opinion (his way of looking at it) that encompassed the points of view of both men. Each would pause and agree with him, and then—in surprise— realize they were agreeing with each other. Mr. Bachman continued this practice, interjecting when necessary, making statements that in fact showed that the points of view being expressed at the table were not contradictory but compatible. Soon, when he said, "Well, let's look at it this way . . ." he had everyone's full attention. Mr. Bachman's easy manner, his ability to get across to the others, and his insightful assessment of the situation established an atmosphere in which everyone got down to work. At the completion of their project, the task force was selected by the president of the company for special commendation.

Very responsive and indirect.   Contrary to the stereotypes noted, we have found that many groups of businessmen tend to be more responsive than direct. Particularly in corporate settings that discourage the expression of individual opinions, many employees have developed a communication pattern that is very attentive to others but that masks their real thoughts and feelings. Occasionally such individuals will allow another to lead for them and they, as a consequence, lower their level of commitment to any outcome of the decision-making processes. Other times, all individuals in a group will operate in this manner, giving everyone the impression that they are operating in limbo, with no firm guidelines or expectations.

In contrast to the noisemakers, individuals who are very re-

Example 6.3 Direct and Unresponsive Communication

In a group meeting, three of the supervisors present were very strong in presenting their opinions—but demonstrated little responsiveness to others. As a consequence, individuals frequently interrupted each other, one scowled and threw up his hands whenever another spoke, and another rarely spoke without pointing a pencil or a finger at the other members of the group. There was little consensus at the table and the one who spoke loudest carried the day. All the group members left the meeting table disgruntled, feeling that they had been done in.

Another group met together over a period of ten weeks. The group was composed of three women and two men. One older woman initially dominated the group, in part, because of her extensive experience in administrative positions. In the first sessions, others listened to this woman's opinions with some interest. As the group moved into the fourth and fifth session, however, there was increasing restlessness among most group members and traces of hostility toward the woman, who continued to dominate the group. At the sixth session, the group was seen for a moment in what became a typical stance. The dominant woman continued to talk. Many of the group members pulled their chairs farther away from her. Almost all of them leaned back with their arms crossed. Several were frowning. Others were tapping pencils. They had clearly closed themselves off to her influence.

---

sponsive and indirect are often *saboteurs,* and their point of view may not be known for a time. Only when a group is supposed to act on a common project is their opinion apparent, more often by what they do not do than what they do. In the face of action, they may demonstrate passive resistance because the agreed-upon plan did not include their own ideas (which were left unstated). Two descriptions of groups characterized by responsiveness without directness are given in Example 6.4.

In summary, effective communication is both very direct and very responsive. Individuals who are direct and *not* responsive may generate a lot of noise and create irritation among their colleagues, but generally carry less weight in decision-making processes than many other individuals. On the other hand, people who are responsive and *not* direct may sabotage group activity because their point of view seldom surfaces until the time for action is near and they will resist accomplishing goals to which they have not agreed. Those people, however, who are both direct and responsive generally become informal leaders in groups and, over time, encourage the

Example 6.4 Indirect and Responsive Communication

The manager of one manufacturing unit was rated highly on listening by his employees. However, the evaluations in other areas were only moderate—and occasionally weak. His employees complained that he did not set clear expectations for them and that they did not know what he wanted them to do. He would listen . . . and listen . . . but did not tell his employees *what he thought* and consequently they often felt that they were walking around as in a swamp, without firm footing.

In a group meeting all members of the table demonstrated very responsive behavior—except one. This one person talked and everybody else listened. They indicated their willingness to listen by leaning across the table, by nodding in response, and by focusing on the one person who spoke most of the time. As this person arrived at a decision, everybody else nodded in agreement. However, when the group dispersed, none of the "responsive" members of the group put aside any time or energy to carry out the decision; they did not feel it was *their* decision but rather *his*—the property of the one person who spoke up during the meeting.

---

development of similar qualities in other group members. Directness and responsiveness of most group members then establish a base of shared expectations from which effective groups operate.

Pyramids and Circles

As group members interact, their shared expectations reflect a common understanding of the purposes of the group. Some groups are brought together primarily to accomplish tasks. Other groups meet primarily to share information. As the expectations of the group focus on a particular purpose, effective groups will assume the particular shape or structure that is appropriate to their purpose. Thus, some groups will become more pyramidal, in order to achieve specific objectives, and some groups will become more circular, in order to share information. The structure that the group adopts will arise from the understanding of the purposes of the group. The structure is, therefore, a function of shared group expectations. However, the structure also will influence those expectations—and the communication that occurs.

Communication in pyramids. Pyramids are designed to get things done, and have a hierarchical structure. Expectations about communication follow from those given. Communication is used appropriately in pyramidal settings to accomplish tasks, to recognize the authority of some, and to give direction and guidance to others. Consequently, communication in pyramids is task-centered and moves along limited channels. Information is relevant to accomplishing goals, implementing procedures and evaluating performance (see Figure 6.2).

Communication in circles.   Circles are designed to share information, and people within such settings have equal power. Expecta-

FIGURE 6.2
COMMUNICATION IN PYRAMIDS AND CIRCLES

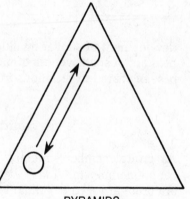

Sender-Receiver Unequal in
Status and Function

Task-Centered and Channeled

Communicating Information
for Task Accomplishment,
Implementing Procedures,
and Evaluating Performance

PYRAMIDS

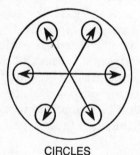

Sender-Receiver Equal
in Status & Function

Personal and Open

Clarify Problems and
Generate Alternatives

CIRCLES

tions about communication are consonant with those characteristics. Communication is appropriate when people are personal and open with each other and speak along a multiplicity of channels, sharing not only facts, information, and ideas but personal experience as well. Information that is communicated in circles is accepted as relevant whatever the nature, for within circles people welcome the experience of others, however idiosyncratic. A variety of viewpoints enhances the group's interaction, enlarging the experience of each member and generating as many new ideas and approaches as possible to any particular problem at hand (see Figure 6.2).

Communication and effective structures. As long as communication in either pyramids or circles is both direct and responsive, group members will share their own expectations and listen to those of others. They will have a shared understanding of the purposes of the group. When the purposes change, the new purposes will be shared and the group will shift their expectations. Consequently, the effectiveness of communication will lead to a clear understanding of purpose—and as purposes shift, the group will take a new shape that is appropriate for new purposes.

Groups that resist information from both within and without, never will clarify new functions and purposes as they emerge both from circumstances within the group and in the outer environment. Such groups become structures of the past, unable to deal with a changing present. Communication is, therefore, the process through which groups maintain their ability to live in and adapt to a changing environment. Communication, in short, maintains the flexibility of any structural formation and allows the structure to adapt to changing circumstances.

Expectations of Up-Down Communication in Pyramids

In the past decade we have focused as a culture on improving circular communication where we are all more or less equal. We have emphasized the importance of sharing our experience and of listening to others share with us. Americans on the whole have focused on the importance of relationships. Many of us have learned how to talk to others in a circular environment.

As organizations once again become the focus of our cultural attention, however, it is clear that we have not always learned to talk to each other when we do not occupy equal positions. With a new emphasis on participative management, bosses are being asked to share information with their employees on a more continual basis. Employees are being asked also to share their ideas, suggestions, and opinions with their bosses. We have to talk with each other, but the labels of hierarchy hang over the door of the communication.

Up-Down Communication

In pyramids, expectations about communication are related to an individual's place within a hierarchy. Expectations for those above differ from those below. Although each individual may be above and below someone else, different expectations will govern his or her behavior, depending on the status relationship in which the communication occurs. Effective communication occurs when individuals, whether above or below, have taken the time to respond to the other's position as well as their own.

From bottom to top. Those on the lower rungs of the organizational ladder are often inhibited from communicating upward for fear of negative evaluations. Often, however, their communication is welcomed—when it is phrased according to the expectations of those above them. In general, there are several specific expectations governing upward communication. Meeting these expectations increases the probability that individuals will be heard (see Figure 6.3).

CONFIRMING STATUS. Speakers fare better when they recognize and confirm the superior status of the other person. Doing so removes fears that the subordinate may be implying, "I can do your job better than you can." Status may be confirmed by both verbal and nonverbal behaviors. Verbal signals include, "Are you busy?" (indicating an awareness of the superior's time constraints); "I appreciated hearing your advice the other day" (indicating an awareness of the value of their ideas); "I know you have the final say" (recognizing their authority); and many others. Nonverbal signals include not intruding on a superior's space without invitation, not gesturing in demanding or evaluative ways, not staring or backing the other down.

FIGURE 6.3
APPROPRIATE COMMUNICATION IN PYRAMIDS

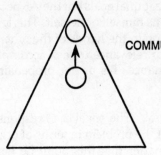

COMMUNICATING RELEVANT INFORMATION

1. Confirmation of Status
2. Identification of Problem
3. Identification of Importance
   of Problem (Why Does He/She
   Want to Know?)
4. Explanation of Alternatives

COMMUNICATING RELEVANT INFORMATION

1. Confirmation of Value to
   Operation
2. Explanation of Decisions
   and Rationale
3. Presentation of All Necessary
   Information Related to Topic
4. Clarity on Procedures and
   Expected Results

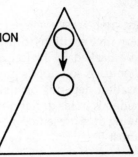

© 1981 Human Systems Analysis, Inc.
Barbara Forisha, Ph.D.

CLARIFYING RELEVANCE. Those speaking to their superiors are responsible for making their communication relevant to the other. Often, immediate concerns of those lower down may appear to be of little interest to their superiors. In general, information that is welcomed is relevant to getting things done. Such information may be important to achieving organizational goals. Much information may indeed fill the bill on this issue, but the speaker has another responsibility. Without wandering, digressing, and moving into personal experiences and emotional accounts, the speaker is responsible for presenting the information in such a way that the relevance to the superior is clear and evident. Sometimes, those lower down enter the office of those higher in the hierarchy with concerns that are relevant to organizational goals but they expect the other person to make the connections himself or herself. This leaves the reception of such communication in the hands of the other. By shaping the communication so that relevance to task accomplishment is apparent, the speaker enhances his or her probability of being heard and understood.

RELATING TO ORGANIZATIONAL OBJECTIVES. The speaker is responsible as well for stating the importance of the problem in terms of organizational objectives. Why does it matter that this point be heard? What difference does it make? What will be the outcome? Is the outcome of measurable import compared to other matters which are pending? Those lower in the organization can be sure that their voice will be listened to when they have important matters to discuss. The phrasing of the matter, and the justification, lies in the hands of the speaker.

PRESENTING ALTERNATIVE SOLUTIONS. The speaker may also propose alternative solutions to any situation discussed. Each solution ought to be backed by logical argument about possible consequences. When each solution is presented, however, the remainder of conversation depends on the person of higher status. What will be decided is in his or her purview and not in that of the subordinate. Having thus presented a good case, the subordinate may relax, for it is most likely that his or her point of view has been received.

From top to bottom. Other expectations govern the behavior of superiors who wish to win the acceptance and engage the motivation of their subordinates.

CONFIRMING PERSONAL VALUE. Superiors are more often heard by their subordinates when they recognize and confirm the value of each person. The superior may indeed be higher in company status but not in human worth. Consequently, when the superior acknowledges the subordinate as a person of merit, it is more likely that each will hear the other. Again, this information may be conveyed by verbal and nonverbal signals. Phrases such as "I'm glad to see you again," "I hear you've been doing good work," "Your opinion has always been helpful," and others indicate receptiveness to the other. Also, nonverbal behaviors such as moving away from a desk, minimizing evaluative gestures, maintaining eye contact, and nodding in response to the other's speech all indicate a receptivity to the other and a recognition of the value of the other person.

EXPLAINING DECISIONS. A high-status person recognizes subordinates as valued members of the work team by explaining decisions to them and giving rationales for behavior. Recognizing that the need to know about matters is a universal desire and not one reserved for high-status individuals validates the other person.

PRESENTING SUFFICIENT INFORMATION. Explanations are enhanced by the presentation of all material relevant to the issue at hand. Presenting sufficient information allows others the opportunity to evaluate and examine decisions as well as to confirm them. In presenting enough information for another to come to his or her conclusions, the high-status person says that the subordinate's thoughts and opinions matter.

CLARIFYING EXPECTATIONS. Communication is improved when superiors are clear in their expectations of others' performance, when they identify procedures and outline expected results. Subordinates then do not run the risk of doing what they think they are supposed to—and discover that it is, in fact, contrary to expectations. Clarifying expectations allows others the chance to think about them and to choose or not choose to meet them. Leaving expectations unclarified leaves others groping in the dark, and only the lucky person, or the one chosen ahead of time, can win.

Communication and Group Effectiveness

Effective communication is based on sharing and acknowledging a common set of expectations among individuals. When such expectations coalesce around a group purpose, the foundation is laid for effective group functioning. Whether in pyramidal or circular structures, the purposes of the group will be met most effectively by individuals who are direct and responsive in communication. Within pyramids, direct and responsive individuals will acknowledge the status of others in the group. Within circles, such individuals will facilitate the open sharing of information among equals. Such individuals become centers of influence within their group and cause others in the group to increase their own degree of influence as well. A group containing many such individuals becomes the focus of change within their organization.

EXERCISE: SAYING WHAT YOU WANT TO SAY

Find one other person with whom to do this exercise. Each of you review the following questions and decide how you would respond to them. When you are ready, share your answers with your partner. Allow one person to speak first. The listener may ask clarifying questions but may not interrupt or evaluate what is being said. When this person is finished speaking, switch roles and have the other person speak while the first one responds.

1. What are the qualities (talents, skills, personality, characteristics) required for success in your current position? Are there areas in which you would like to learn new patterns of behavior? Do you have particular talents for which you would like more recognition?
2. What would you like to see change in your work environment in the next two years? five years? Do you think it is possible for these changes to occur? What can you do to see that they happen?
3. Imagine that you were going to retire in the next ten years. At this imaginary retirement party, your employees write a speech about you that describes their real opinion of you. What do you think they would say? What would you like them to say? Is there a difference? What can you do to be the kind of supervisor you would like to be?

When you have finished speaking, evaluate your own communication and that of your partner according to the following scale:

Nonverbal Behavior Observation Scale

Place a number from 0 to 3 in each space (0 is low, 3 is high), indicating the degree to which you think you and your partner demonstrated the following behaviors:

	Self	Partner
Spoke clearly	_____	_____
Looked other in the eye	_____	_____
Faced other directly	_____	_____
Sat in a relaxed manner	_____	_____
Gestured for emphasis	_____	_____
Spoke with expression	_____	_____
Leaned forward	_____	_____
Nodded in response	_____	_____
Smiled	_____	_____
Total (+)	_____	_____
Mumbled	_____	_____
Looked away	_____	_____
Turned away	_____	_____
Crossed arms	_____	_____
Tapped, jiggled, or twitched	_____	_____
Yelled or spoke in monotone	_____	_____
Leaned back	_____	_____
Pointed fingers or pencils	_____	_____
Scowled, frowned, or grimaced	_____	_____
Total (−)	_____	_____
CHANGE CAPABILITY = Total (+) Total (−) =	_____	_____

If your score is between 18 and 27, you demonstrate HIGH Change Capability and are probably a "CENTER OF INFLUENCE" in your environment.

If your score is between 9 and 18, you demonstrate MODERATE Change Capability and are only occasionally a "CENTER OF INFLUENCE" in your environment.

If your score is below 9, you demonstrate LOW Change Capability and are only rarely a "CENTER OF INFLUENCE" in your environment.

(For further information on the interpretation of your scores see *Organizational Sync.*)

7
Group Norms and Expectations and the Change Process

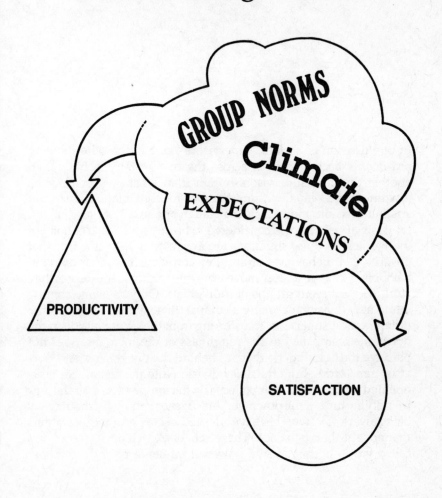

GROUP NORMS

Climate

EXPECTATIONS

PRODUCTIVITY

SATISFACTION

In one division of a plant, supervisors "zing" each other, yelling put-downs back and forth across the roar of the machinery. In another division, supervisors refrain from what they perceive as rowdiness and keep their conversations focused on the task. In still another division, individuals may laugh and joke but only quietly, for raising one's voice is considered to be in poor taste. Yet none of the workers in these situations are aware of any specific rule that governs their behavior, nor are they conscious that their own behavior may change as they move from one setting to the next as they work with different groups of individuals. Only someone coming into a new division or taking a comparative survey recognizes the differences. A supervisor transferring from the quiet division to the noisy one is appalled at the roughness of the men and does not perceive the camaraderie that lies behind the put-downs. A supervisor transferring from the noisy division into the restrained, task-oriented one is equally appalled at what he perceives as the unfriendly attitude of the other workers. In each setting, without really being aware of it, workers have adopted a set of group expectations that govern their behavior. These sets of expectations, sometimes called group norms, exert a powerful influence on individual behavior. If individuals and organizations are going to change, group norms also have to change.

Group Norms

Group norms have been defined in a variety of ways. Group norms may be made explicit in rules, regulations, or procedures. More often, group norms are implicit—not verbalized. Organizational members may not even be aware of certain group norms or of the ways in which they shape individual behavior. Existing on the implicit level, group norms have been referred to as customs or traditions. Although events may be interpreted in terms of these norms, the reasons why one interpretation is accepted over another may not be understood. Rather, it is assumed that "this is the way things are." Alfred Schutz, a German sociologist, has described the operation of group norms as "thinking-as-usual," a way of being and operating that is seldom questioned.

Group norms are, in fact, shared group expectations that have been accepted over time. Originally, group norms emerge from the expectations of initial members of any group. Those who begin a group share their own expectations and arrive at a set of consensual expectations, which become the "thinking-as-usual" by which the group conducts its business. Those who are more influential in the group (that is, who are more direct and responsive) carry the greatest weight in terms of shaping the original expectations. As the group itself develops a history, these norms become an implicit part of that history. As new members enter the group, their expectations, over time, also have an impact on strengthening or redirecting existing group norms (see Figure 7.1).

Group expectations include the beliefs about how people should act in all situations and, as such, have a strong impact on individual behavior. Groups that have been successful in meeting their own expectations—and accomplishing their stated goals—often are tolerant in the application of their beliefs about individual behavior. Such groups may tolerate more deviance among group members. Groups, on the other hand, that have been unsuccessful in attaining goals tend to tighten their control over individual behavior, as if the increased cohesiveness and apparent similarity of group members may compensate for lack of success in other ways.

FIGURE 7.1
GROUP EXPECTATIONS AND
THE ORGANIZATIONAL CONTEXT

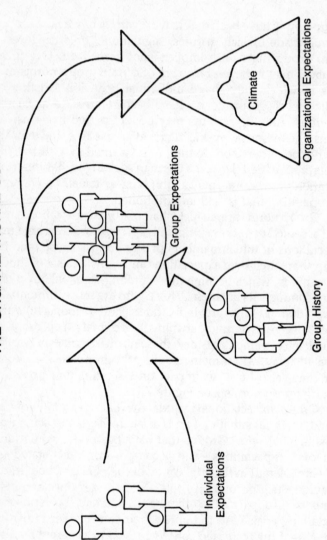

Individual Expectations

Group History

Group Expectations

Climate

Organizational Expectations

As groups live out their expectations, and affect the behavior of group members, they carry their experience of the past into the future.

Group Climate

Group norms or expectations also form the climate of the organization. Many groups, operating together, tend to shape the atmosphere of the organization and, to a large extent, influence the productivity and satisfaction of all individuals in the workplace. Climate has been defined as the set of shared perceptions or expectations of individual members of an organization. Climate, therefore, can also be defined as the shared perceptions or expectations of different groups within the organization, the group being the intermediary between the individual and the total system. Thus, group expectations not only affect the individuals but also the tone or atmosphere of the total organization, and, in fact, provide the framework for the informal operation of that system.

The climate of an organization is permeated with the unspoken expectations of that organization. The climate, in effect, is the unseen force that establishes standards of conduct, encourages individuals to respond to what is seen as deviant behavior, and encourages individuals to reward behavior that is in accord with the implicit expectations. The shared perceptions and expectations within an organization thus regularize patterns of behavior, disciplining those that are not accepted and rewarding those that are. Thus, behavior within organizations, over time, becomes predictable as people move in the patterns established by the group norms.

The climate also acts as a filter that allows certain information in and keeps other information out. Data that is not congruent with implicit expectations may be rejected, distorted, or not heard. Data that is in accord with the beliefs of group members will be circulated among the group (see Figure 7.2). The degree to which the organization is effective in maintaining a set of unwritten rules will, to some extent, determine the cohesiveness of groups within the organization, and affect the degree to which groups will be effective or ineffective. The effectiveness of the groups, however, will depend not only on acceptance of group norms, but on the constructive or

FIGURE 7.2
CLIMATE EFFECTS

Effect on Individual	Effect on Group
1) Control	1) Regularize Patterns
2) Discipline	for Individual and Group
3) Patterns for Behavior	2) Determine Cohesiveness
	3) Filter Information

destructive nature of these norms in respect to organizational purposes.

Constructive and Destructive Group Norms

Group norms that encourage the accomplishment of tasks and the sharing of information may be regarded as constructive within an organizational context. Within pyramidal structures, group norms focusing on accomplishment will be more important; and within circular structures, norms that encourage the dissemination of information will be critical to group effectiveness. In either structure, group expectations that facilitate getting things done and sharing with others are essential to effective group functioning.

Constructive group norms in either setting focus on the purpose of the group. Destructive group norms focus on the appearance of the group—and the appearance of control. In pyramidal group settings, constructive group norms will reward those who accomplish tasks and discipline those who do not. In contrast, destructive group norms will reward those who appear to be getting things done because they have higher status or more control over others. In circular group settings, constructive group norms will reward those who share openly with the group and are responsive to others. On the other hand, destructive group norms will reward those who appear to be sharing with others only because they spend more time in the group setting or because they never say anything with which someone might disagree. In short, constructive group norms require that members focus on the task at hand, whereas destructive group norms aid members in avoiding confrontation with the immediate tasks and purposes that further organizational goals.

Group Norms and the Process of Change

In order for individuals and organizations to change, the norms that govern the behavior of individuals must also change. Individuals who change their behavior in ways that contradict group norms or expectations will call down upon themselves the disapproval of the group. New behavior by individuals will be regarded as strange or unusual and likely to lead to a bad end. Consequently, in order for new behavior to be accepted, group norms must change to tolerate these new behaviors. In like manner, organizational edicts about changes in procedures, policies, and style, will run afoul of group norms that are not in accord with the new ways of being. Groups will only pay lip service to new organizational goals, and unless the unspoken group norms change, individual members will do likewise and subvert any efforts to actually implement new procedures.

Therefore, any effort at organizational change requires that the underlying assumptions of the organization, and of its composite groups, be analyzed and brought into awareness. This is not a simple process, since patterns of behavior that have been unquestioned and that are believed to be "simply the way things are" are not easily recognized nor challenged. The process of changing group expectations proceeds in many stages, as individuals within organizations come to recognize, accept, and act to change the group norms that are not compatible with current individual and organizational goals.

Awareness and Recognition of Group Norms

Several questions provide a guide to increasing awareness and recognition of the group expectations that govern behavior in any group. The questions are *What* is happening in the group? *How* is it happening? and *Why* is it happening? Focusing on each of these questions in turn will lead to a greater awareness of group norms and the effects that they have on guiding individual behavior in groups.

What is happening?   Individuals often do not see what is happening around them, rather they see what they expect to see. If, for a time, they are asked to focus on actual behavior and to describe that behavior specifically, they are likely to go beyond their expectations to observe what is actually transpiring in their environment. As individuals note specific behaviors, and chronicle events without interpretation, they will begin to describe the patterns of behavior that actually occur in their group. As they do so, they will also increase their skill in observation and listening and sensitize themselves to behaviors and more subtle cues that indicate the direction of events in their group. For example, in observing communication processes within a group, individuals may note which parties talk most, to whom, and in what order. Their observations will be a record of *what* is happening in the communication (see Figure 7.3).

How is it happening?   Observation of how people communicate with each other will add further information about group interaction. How do people make contacts with each other? How do they speak to each other? Does their conversation indicate openness, rejection, restraint, aggression, warmth, or anger? With minimal interpretation, individuals learn from noting the actual language patterns, the verbal and nonverbal behavior, and the tone of what is occurring. Figure 7.4 shows how communication may be inter-

FIGURE 7.3
IDENTIFYING GROUP NORMS I

What Is Happening?

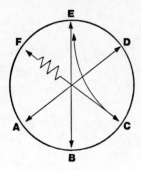

Who talks most?
Who supports whom?
Who interrupts whom?

preted within the framework of effective and ineffective pyramids and circles.

Why is it happening? To answer this question requires some further interpretation. As observers of human behavior, we may see what happens around us. With a little interpretation, we may describe how it happens. Then, from our knowledge of ourselves and others, we may form hypotheses about why people behave as they do. We cannot see why things happen, but we may make certain assumptions about causality. If we assume that there are logical explanations for most behavior, we can approximate the whys of behavior by postulating the reasons why some pattern of behavior is occurring. When we have eliminated individual idiosyncrasies, our explanations will, in fact, give us a clue to the norms which govern behavior in any particular setting. Figure 7.5 suggests some common reasons why certain behavior occurs within pyramidal and circular frameworks.

FIGURE 7.4
IDENTIFYING GROUP NORMS II
How Is It Happening?

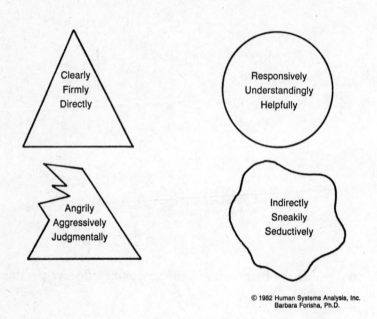

Clearly
Firmly
Directly

Responsively
Understandingly
Helpfully

Angrily
Aggressively
Judgmentally

Indirectly
Sneakily
Seductively

Evaluation of Old Norms
and Implementation of New Ones

When individuals ask what, how, and why, old norms surface and may be evaluated and replaced with new ones. In Example 7.1, an engineer asks "Why?" and discovers that a familiar expectation may be changed at considerable savings to the company. In Example 7.2, another group of people discover that their familiar expectations of each other, which continually lead to friction between groups, may be changed by sharing information across groups. As groups observe and then interpret their own behavior, they turn up information on which to base new and more constructive decisions. In each case, groups may *evaluate* group norms, *target* norms for change, and *implement* new norms.

FIGURE 7.5

IDENTIFYING GROUP NORMS III

Why Is It Happening?

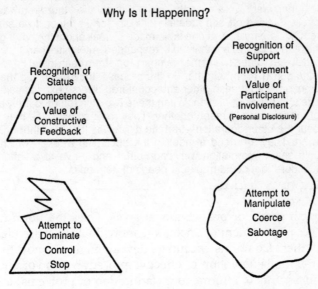

Recognition of
Status
Competence
Value of
Constructive
Feedback

Recognition of
Support
Involvement
Value of
Participant
Involvement
(Personal Disclosure)

Attempt to
Dominate
Control
Stop

Attempt to
Manipulate
Coerce
Sabotage

© 1981 Human Systems Analysis, Inc.
Barbara Forisha, Ph.D.

Evaluation of group norms. Once people have identified why events occur as they do or individuals behave as they do, they have come close to identifying a group norm. They may then evaluate this norm by asking whether or not the norm helps the group to ac-

Example 7.1 Changing Group Norms I

"One man for each machine" was one of the unwritten rules in the production area of an industrial company. As the engineers in the company began to look at ways to cut costs, one of them questioned this rule. "Why," he asked, "can't one man run two machines?" "Because he can't see two machines at once," was the familiar and expected answer. The questioning engineer then suggested, that in several areas of the plant, machines that ran alternately with each other be turned around to face the same worker and be monitored as part of the same job. In each instance that this occurred, the company saved one person's salary without overtaxing the remaining worker.

Example 7.2 Changing Group Norms II

Group expectations between two different functional areas in a manufacturing plant were such that each thought the other area was purposely slacking off and creating difficulty for the other. In a seminar meeting, supervisors at one table made a crack about the other group. The other group, at another table, responded. After initial barrages were fired at each other, two of the members (one from each table) headed off to the coffee room together. In the process, they examined their assumptions about each other and countered diverse expectations with facts about their operation. When these two men returned, they asked both their tables to meet together. They realized how little they knew about the other operation—and the difficulties that the other unit was facing. They arranged a meeting the upcoming week in which they could share information with each other and arrive at a scheduling procedure that could meet the needs of both units.

---

complish group or organizational goals. Does the norm facilitate task accomplishment or encourage individuals to share ideas with each other? Do norms encourage development of innovative ideas and the implementation of effective procedures and/or encourage openness to new information, clarification of problems, and a responsiveness to and trust in others? In contrast, one might ask if the norms encourage malingering on the job, repress innovation, hamper the implementation process, limit communication, prevent analysis of problems, and encourage the development of fear as opposed to trust.

Some norms facilitate task accomplishment and are characteristic of effective pyramids. Other norms facilitate a smooth information flow and are characteristic of effective circles (see Figure 7.6). Effective organizations as a whole include both effective pyramids and effective circles—and organizational expectations will be supported by group norms that reward getting things done and create a sense of belonging among group members. The result of such a set of expectations is an organizational climate that furthers productivity and satisfaction.

Targeting group norms for change. After group norms are evaluated, some of those that are counterproductive in terms of organizational goals may be targeted for change. For each target norm, the behavior, the process, and the rationale for that behavior can be

FIGURE 7.6
EVALUATING GROUP NORMS

DO GROUP NORMS:

1) Facilitate

Getting
Work
Done?

Innovation?

Implementing
Effective
Procedures?

Maximizing Output
from Limited Resources?

2) Facilitate

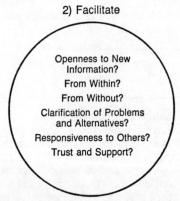

Openness to New
Information?

From Within?

From Without?

Clarification of Problems
and Alternatives?

Responsiveness to Others?

Trust and Support?

clarified. Strategies for change may then be selected that will reinforce a set of behaviors different from those previously reinforced. In Example 7.3, supervisors chose to revise expectations about daily cleanup and devised a new system of rewards for those who performed this function well. In Example 7.4, another group of supervisors encouraged the development of responsibility among a larger group of workers by allowing more of them to participate in interesting tasks, which was seen as a reward in itself. In each case, the

105

group of individuals who instigated the change made a commitment to focusing their time and energy during the initial period of transition in implementing new behavior—aware that in the long run they too would profit from the change in group expectations.

Example 7.3 Changing Group Norms III

A group of supervisors in a technical area of a manufacturing plant sat together for several hours examining the group norms that shaped behavior in their unit. They quickly identified a set of group norms that allowed their men to get away with "bad housekeeping." As a consequence, at the end of each of their shifts they were continually picking up for their men, putting equipment away, and getting the area ready for the next shift. The expectation of their men was that, regardless of their own behavior, their supervisors would cover for them by getting the unit clean for the incoming shift. The supervisors agreed to set up a new system in which they would put their energies, not into picking up, but into monitoring cleanup crews among the men. They also devised a system of rewards to honor the crews that did the best job. Instituting the new norms required a commitment of time and energy from all the supervisors. However, the early period of more intense effort on their part led, in the long term, to a more efficient and less taxing cleanup procedure.

Example 7.4 Changing Group Norms IV

Within a production area of a manufacturing plant, several supervisors recognized that they were perceived as playing favorites because they relied for assistance continually on subordinates whom they thought were the most responsible and capable. They realized, however, in thinking this through, that the result was they had developed over the years one group of subordinates. In relying on this group, they were not taking the time to develop other talent that might exist among their workers. Consequently, they decided that each of them, in selecting individuals to assist in responsible positions, would select only two out of three from the groups that had previously proven themselves and would select one out of three from the rest of their workers. Choosing a majority from the known group would insure satisfactory performance and provide a check on new people being given responsibility. However, choosing one person from other groups would give other talent a chance to surface. In effect, without thinking much about it, they *had* played favorites by not offering opportunities to those who were newer in the organization. As they instituted their plan, the notion that they played favorites began to dissipate.

In another case, workers had so much difficulty analyzing group expectations within the organization that they backed up to focus on why it was so difficult for them to uncover shared expectations, or, in other words, why they did not perceive group norms in the same way. Consequently, their plan of action involved breaking down the specializations that had kept them isolated in different areas of the plant. The basic norm that they targeted for change was an expectation of specialization, which blocked communication flow among workers in different areas (see Example 7.5).

Example 7.5 Changing Group Norms V

Several employees of one plant met in a group to arrive together at some plans by which they could improve the functioning of their organization. As they talked about the expectations of their organization, they realized that each of them viewed these expectations from an entirely different perspective. One individual was a first-line supervisor who worked on the afternoon shift, and another worked in a specialty department on the day shift. Two other individuals were in higher-status positions in staff jobs—personnel and quality assurance.

As they had difficulty agreeing on the norms that governed their plant, they realized that one central expectation was at the root of their difficulty. Like many American industrial organizations, they were each adhering to a group norm emphasizing the importance of specialization of function. Because they were specialized, either in terms of shifts or functions, they were unable to perceive other expectations in the same light as each other. Consequently, they examined the group expectation that they would remain in their separate functions and found there was no overt regulation that said that they must do so.

Their plan, now put in operation, is to view the organization from each other's perspective at least once by "walking in each other's shoes" for one day. Each member of this group is now taking the other's position for one day, and then they will meet, and from enhanced perspectives, work on clarifying other norms of the organization.

In each case, individuals examined what was occurring in their work setting, how it was occurring, and why it was occurring. They then identified group norms that explained *why* something was happening, and evaluated the constructive or destructive effect of these norms. Then they targeted one group norm for change.

Implementing strategies for change. Finally, individuals in groups begin the process of implementing new group norms. Sometimes the implementation is a simple process, such as reversing one of the machines on the floor of a plant. Sometimes the process is more difficult, such as establishing new expectations for good housekeeping among a technical crew. Other times the norms may take years to implement, such as breaking down barriers between functions that have arisen over years and that are based upon an expectation that specialization leads to effectiveness. Groups may begin this process, as in the examples, by establishing meetings between groups, by changing roles, or by interchanging functions for a day. But spreading the process throughout a whole plant will take time. The process of change is almost always slow and the first step is the most difficult. However, each group described in the examples took the first step, which began a larger process of change. A summary description of this process is given in Figure 7.7.

Group Norms and the Process of Change

Any change in individual or organizational behavior will require a change in the norms that govern behavior within any group or organization. The composite set of group expectations, in fact, establishes the climate of that organization, that intangible pervasive atmosphere strongly related to both satisfaction and productivity. When individuals act so as to change group norms, the process by which they enact change will evolve through several steps, which can be restated as follows:

1. Identify current behavior and events.
2. Identify process by which behavior and events occurs.
3. Determine the most likely rationale for both the observed behaviors/events and the process by which they are carried out (identify norms).
4. Evaluate the norms in terms of their usefulness in facilitating task accomplishment or group identification.
5. Create new norms to replace nonfunctional ones and develop the systems of feedback and reinforcement to institute these changes.
6. Implement, over time, the new group norms, periodically evaluating progress toward this goal.

The implications of any change in group norms will have effects beyond the immediate group involved and will affect the organizational system in such a way as to provoke change in other groups as well.

FIGURE 7.7

CHANGING GROUP NORMS

1) IDENTIFY BEHAVIOR: What is done?
2) IDENTIFY PROCESS: How is it done?
3) IDENTIFY RATIONALE: Why is it done?

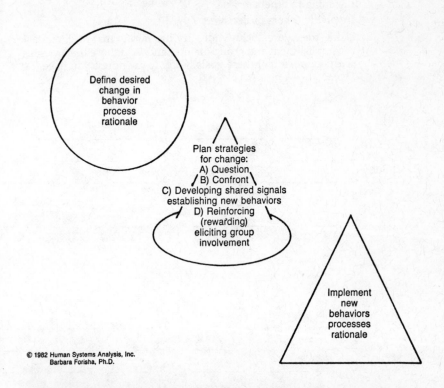

© 1982 Human Systems Analysis, Inc.
Barbara Forisha, Ph.D.

EXERCISE: GROUP NORMS

A. Write down all the expectations for behavior (group norms) that exist within your work group. If you have difficulty identifying group norms, spend some time observing people at work and ask What? How? and Why? about the events that you observe. Consider all areas of your work setting. Consideration of some of the following areas may help you further in identifying group norms.

Areas in which most groups have informal group norms:

Recognition of status	Responsiveness to personal disclosure
Rewards for competence	
Value of constructive feedback	Maintaining control and discipline
Means of feedback to each other	Displaying opposition
	Allowing sabotage
Support for others	Coercing colleagues
Listening to others	Winning
Involving others in decisions	Losing

B. Using the figures below, identify the norms that facilitate task accomplishment and group maintenance and those that interfere with the pursuit of these goals. Refer to the norms you have just listed.

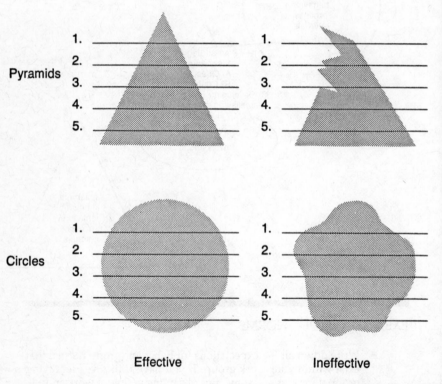

Pyramids

1. _____
2. _____
3. _____
4. _____
5. _____

1. _____
2. _____
3. _____
4. _____
5. _____

Circles

1. _____
2. _____
3. _____
4. _____
5. _____

1. _____
2. _____
3. _____
4. _____
5. _____

Effective

Ineffective

C. As a group, select one norm operational in your work setting that you will target for change.

If a number of norms are interrelated and you desire to change all of them, they may all be listed. One norm, however, should receive highest priority.

1. Write down your norm selected for change. List other related norms.
2. Identify new norm(s) to be established in its (their) place.
3. What steps would you take to implement this change?
4. What would be the short- and long-term benefits of this change?

Guiding
the Change Process
in Problem Solving
and Decision Making

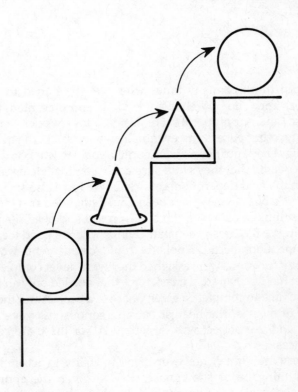

We all can think of many times when we have tried to change something and failed. We had a good idea and presented it to our supervisor and our proposal sat on his desk for a week before it got lost among other papers and eventually was found in the trash can. Or we might have got people in our unit to come to work on time and then discovered that they were once again coming late because the people in the next department came late. We have also sat in meetings where a boss (it may have been you) demanded that the group members think of new ideas for some project and dead silence was the result. We have also been in meetings where a good idea never got off the floor because nobody could decide who would do what—or if functions were assigned they were never completed. Or we might have been part of a task force that needed only an hour or two more time to complete a given phase of a project and the group decided to meet at the nearest bar and seriousness gave way to joviality and the project was forgotten. All of these are common occurrences.

Every individual, however, has the ability to accomplish almost anything he or she chooses to do—given the appropriate commitment of time and energy. All of us have the capacity to shape the process of change. In order, however, to move successfully through the change process we need to understand the different phases of the process and establish the appropriate structure for each stage. The process of change is multifaceted and can be described in discrete stages, although the behaviors of each stage may often overlap and intermix. Difficulties in the change process may occur because individuals do not recognize the different purposes of each stage and do not adopt the appropriate structures, norms, and behaviors to facilitate completion of each stage. In this chapter we shall identify important behaviors and expectations that accompany the process of change and serve as aids to any individuals reaching an impasse in their own individual or organizational change process.

The Time Line of Change

The change process can be placed along a time line, with three stages recycled over time (see Figure 8.1). The first stage is symbolized by a circle, since its primary purpose is to explore the nature of the problem, to clarify underlying assumptions about the problem, and to generate alternative solutions. The second stage is symbolized by a cone, for its purpose is to sift through ideas until an ultimate plan is selected. It requires both an openness to ideas and an ability to evaluate those ideas. The third stage is symbolized by a pyramid, for at this stage in the change process, openness to ideas and information is less important. A plan has been decided upon and is to be put into action. This stage then is an implementation phase. As the process begins a new cycle, the pyramid yields to the circle as one reevaluates whatever has been done.

The Circular Phase

The initial phases of any change process benefit from as much information as possible. Suppose you want to change your own style of supervision. You go out and ask other people what is effective for them, you read books and articles, and perhaps take a class in management behavior. You, in fact, collect as much information as possible about alternative patterns of behavior. The same

FIGURE 8.1
PROBLEM-SOLVING AND DECISION-MAKING TIMELINE

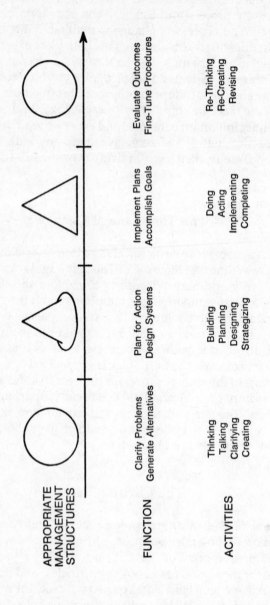

APPROPRIATE
MANAGEMENT
STRUCTURES

FUNCTION

Clarify Problems
Generate Alternatives

Plan for Action
Design Systems

Implement Plans
Accomplish Goals

Evaluate Outcomes
Fine-Tune Procedures

ACTIVITIES

Thinking
Talking
Clarifying
Creating

Building
Planning
Designing
Strategizing

Doing
Acting
Implementing
Completing

Re-Thinking
Re-Creating
Revising

© 1982 Human Systems Analysis, Inc.
Barbara Forisha, Ph.D.
Randy Kovach, B.S.

holds true if individuals wish to change a group or an organization. It is necessary to gather as much information as possible so that one has examined a wide range of alternatives and has information to assess their viability. The change process begins by casting as wide a net as possible to draw in relevant information.

Since the focus of this stage is collecting information, the best structure for this stage is the circle. A circle encourages communication and establishes expectations that all individuals are valuable and that their ideas will be heard. Visually, a circle is spread flat against the ground and thus is able to draw into itself information from many points of contact with the environment. Within itself, the flatness of the structure allows information to move in all directions. As information is collected, individuals within the circle use the information to clarify the nature of the problem. As the problem is examined from different sides, different forms of solutions will emerge. Some of these alternative solutions will follow past practices and standard procedures. Others will be more innovative in nature. Some may be humorous or off the wall. However, the initial period of any problem-solving or change process is designed to welcome and examine multiple inputs—before subjecting them to the screens and filters of the later stages (see Figure 8.2).

The Conical Phase

The screens and funnels appear in the second stage, in which input is welcomed and evaluated. Each suggestion is scrutinized to assess its possible outcomes and the possibility of implementation. The result of this scrutiny is the development of a viable and significant plan of action. In many ways, this is the most important of all stages, for good planning will minimize error and speed implementation. There are three substages of this second stage (see Figure 8.3).

Sifting alternatives. A definition of the problem must be agreed upon and alternative strategies identified. Two procedures are essential in this process. The first is to evaluate possible outcomes of any alternative solution and to assess the *significance* of these outcomes. Are efforts being bent toward a worthwhile goal? What are the short-range effects? What are the long-range effects? What units will be involved? What will be the short- and long-range effects on

FIGURE 8.2
CIRCULAR PHASE

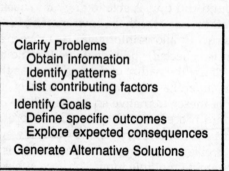

Clarify Problems
    Obtain information
    Identify patterns
    List contributing factors
Identify Goals
    Define specific outcomes
    Explore expected consequences
Generate Alternative Solutions

resources? The exploration of all possible outcomes of the change process will prevent any surprises from occurring in the later process of implementation and keep energies focused on worthwhile outcomes during the planning stage. The significance filter is one of two screens through which to sift alternative strategies.

The second filter involves testing significant ideas for *feasibility* or the possibility of actual implementation. Many worthwhile projects die before they can begin because the resources for implementation are not at hand. Other times, individuals give up change projects altogether because they do not believe that it is possible to implement any of them. Actually, it is usually possible to implement at least part of a significant idea. Sometimes taking the first step is nearly as good as doing it all.

In testing an idea for feasibility there are a number of questions that need to be considered. Is it possible to carry this idea out with existing resources? If not, can the resources be obtained from other

FIGURE 8.3
CONICAL PHASE

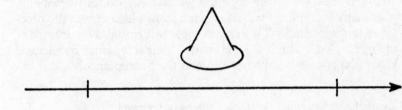

```
PRIORITIZING
      Select Problem and Alternative
          Determine significance
          Determine feasibility
      Re-evaluate Problem and Alternative

DELEGATION
      Develop Strategy
          Break out action steps
          Assign individual responsibility
          Elicit commitment

ACCOUNTABILITY
      Design Evaluation Measures
          Establish
          Create feedback channels
          Plan contingencies
```

areas? Specifically, what resources are necessary to carry out this plan? How much time (an important resource) will be involved? Having identified the resources necessary for implementation, identify the persons who control these resources. Are these people likely to be favorable to this idea?

Every plan then requires that others either approve of or accept the idea in order for implementation to be successful. What other people are going to be involved? Can the necessary resources be easily obtained? If not, can you seek out other avenues? (See Example 8.1.) Have you created an idea that requires the approval of a multitude of individuals? (See Example 8.2.) If so, how could the idea be revised so that fewer people would have to approve? Finally, how many individuals will be affected by this idea during the process of implementation? When will these individuals be informed of the idea? (See Example 8.3.) How will their acceptance be elicited? What procedures will be used to win their acceptance?

Example 8.1 Seeking Alternative Sources of Approval

One group of women managers in a large communications company was working to get a new form of performance appraisal adopted in the system. Faced with a personnel manager whose approval they thought (probably correctly) would not be forthcoming, they became very discouraged. However, prodded by one of the women, they began to examine other alternatives. After a thorough examination of the personnel office, they decided on one person, with considerable clout, who might be able to help them. They delegated two of the managers to approach this person the next day with a well-prepared plan and to ask for her help and advice.

Example 8.2 Requiring Approval from too Many Sources

One group of supervisors in a testing area was faced with what they regarded as a major problem. Because their "customers" from other areas of the company failed to fill out completely the appropriate order forms for a variety of tests, often tests were delayed while information was sought from individuals who were frequently difficult to find. In order to clean up their own operation, the testing supervisors wanted to enforce a policy of completely filling out the order forms. As they moved through the planning stages, they realized that enforcing such an order would eventually require the approval of 12 vice-presidents of the other units. Overcome with the impossibility of the task, they gave up altogether and resigned themselves to an ineffective situation.

When questions about resources, approval, and acceptance of an idea have been satisfactorily answered, the idea is starting to approach becoming an actual plan. Selecting a strategy and drawing up a plan occur in the next stages of the conical process.

Example 8.3 Failing to Elicit Acceptance from Affected Parties

---

A woman executive proposed a new reorganization of her service unit. She calculated resources and talked with her superiors about the possibilities. She received their tentative approval before broaching it with her immediate subordinates within her own unit. In an extended meeting, they suggested revisions for the plan but were basically enthusiastic about the proposal. As final signatures for implementation were being accepted, her boss casually mentioned the plan to four of her peers at a business luncheon. All of them quickly sat back in their chairs, scowled, and started voicing their objections. The woman executive was astonished. She hadn't thought that their response would be so intense or their objections so vehement. She hadn't thought that they would be affected at all.

Devising a strategy.   Much of the planning will evolve from having clearly evaluated the feasibility of the idea. If the feasibility of the project has been carefully explored, it is relatively easy to answer the following questions that must be confronted during this stage of the planning process:

> What steps need to be accomplished to implement this plan?
>
> Where in the time line of your plan must specific resources be acquired?
>
> At what point is it necessary to elicit the approval of key figures?
>
> When and how will you seek the acceptance of other individuals who will be at least peripherally affected by the implementation of this plan?

The answers to these questions will then outline the overall strategy for a proposed change project.

The specific planning stages follow. Specific steps must be outlined and placed along a time line. Individuals who will be accountable for accomplishing each step must be noted. Time must be allotted not only for implementing steps themselves but for contacting all the individuals whose approval and acceptance will lead to the success of the proposed plan. Finally, as this substage concludes, those most centrally involved in the planning process must give their commitment to the plan. Any objections or reservations should be brought to the surface, so that the concluding plan is well supported by all involved in its design.

Planning for evaluation. The last part of the planning process involves designing the specific measures by which progress toward goal completion will be evaluated. How will progress be measured? By whom? When? How will information flow through the entire group so that all central figures are aware of the progress of this project? (See Example 8.4.) Finally, what contingency measures are built in, in order to sidestep obstacles when they occur? With a time line of action steps, with responsibility allocated, feedback measures designed, and with contingency measures in place, the planning stage is concluded.

Example 8.4 Failing to Establish Feedback Channels

One manufacturing unit of a major corporation turned its people loose in what they believed to be participative management style by giving each of several units complete control of their production. When a central figure was asked, "How is it going?" he replied, "How the hell do I know how it's going! Everybody's just doing their own thing!"

The Pyramidal Stage

Ideas that pass successfully through the screening process of the conical stage are likely to result in plans with a strong possibility of successful implementation as they move into the pyramidal phase (see Figure 8.4). The implementation stage is symbolized by the pyramid, since individuals are intent on accomplishing tasks that have already been selected. In this phase, groups may be bogged down by maintaining wide-open information-gathering structures. The time for gathering information has passed and the time for action has come.

When the planning stage has been completed thoroughly, this stage proceeds quickly—and without too many surprises. Feedback channels to communicate progress are operationalized, individual achievements are assessed and noted, and progress toward the objective is monitored. Contingency plans may be brought into operation if and when an obstacle is encountered.

The resulting process from beginning to end can be symbolized by a fluid interaction of circles, cones, and pyramids within the

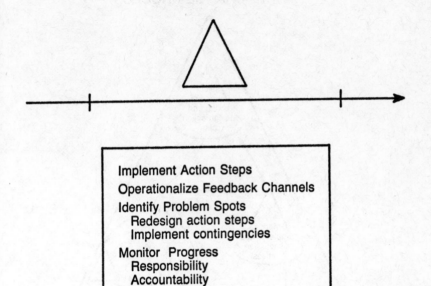

FIGURE 8.4
PYRAMIDAL PHASE

Implement Action Steps
Operationalize Feedback Channels
Identify Problem Spots
  Redesign action steps
  Implement contingencies
Monitor Progress
  Responsibility
  Accountability

organizational structure (see Figure 8.5). Circles begin the process and yield to cones; cones give way to pyramids; and pyramids again to circles. As each structure is suited to the function, circles, cones, and pyramids appear and disappear. The flexibility of the structures is essential to effective monitoring of the change process. One attempt at implementing this procedure through several levels of management is given in Example 8.5.

Shaping the Change Process

The change process is similar whether individuals are concerned with a specific problem, a difficult work relationship, or responding to the shocks generated by environmental change. In any case,

FIGURE 8.5
CIRCLES, CONES AND PYRAMIDS
IN THE CHANGE PROCESS

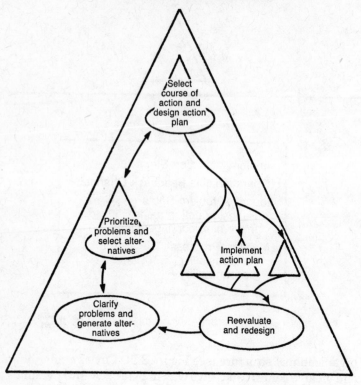

individuals have the option of resigning themselves to distressing situations, adapting themselves to restrictive circumstances, or guiding the process of change toward a constructive conclusion. Individuals always can do something. What and how much they can do, is very much a result of their situation. However, doing something—creating a constructive plan and implementing it—puts control of the change process back in the hands of the individuals involved.

Example 8.5 Implementing the Change Process

In one plant of a major company with a strong participative philosophy, the following procedures were used when two of the larger sections of the plant were required to cut their costs by 15 percent. All supervisory personnel met with their workers for several hours explaining the situation to them and eliciting any suggestions that they might have. Then the supervisors from the two units met in two groups and each developed one alternative strategy that fit with their own needs. They estimated changes in costs, productivity and employee morale that would result from the implementation of their strategy over a year's time. The two general supervisors then presented their units' plans to the top management team. Following their presentation, the top management team retired to arrive at a final decision that incorporated the input of the two units involved. They agreed beforehand that they would not move forward with a plan without the acceptance of the two general supervisors.

The day following the general supervisors' presentations to the management team, the team presented its own strategy to all the individuals in the units involved. The units met with each other and decided on the degree to which they would "buy in" to management's plan. Recognizing that management had either incorporated their own point of view or taken the time to explain why they had rejected various points, they came back to the next meeting to give management a show of support.

Tasks were then assigned to change procedures, and to increase employee training and morale. Individual supervisors were each responsible for part of the larger program. Charts were mounted on the wall to show weekly records of costs and productivity. All of the individuals involved knew where they were going and why—and that their jobs depended on causing the productivity chart to climb and the cost chart to fall. They gave their best efforts to their jobs, exulting over rises in productivity when they occurred. The outcome of their efforts is still not known, as the decision point is still several months away.

EXERCISE: PROBLEM SOLVING IN ORGANIZATIONS

Read the story about the personal difficulties of Jim and Dave on the next pages. Use the following sheets to clarify alternatives for solving their interpersonal problem.

Jim and Dave both had the same position in two different divisions of a corporation. Both of them had the task of relaying reports between divisions and exchanging supplies and products on a regular schedule. Generally, they met together once a week to go over schedules and reports and to coordinate the efforts of the two divisions. For several years they had worked amicably together and people referred to them as a great team, since their work went without a hitch.

At the time our story takes place, however, it became clear to Jim's manager, Mark, that a change had taken place. Jim and Dave met only irregularly, schedules had been interrupted, and occasionally supplies had not been available for the production schedule. One man had commented to Mark that he'd seen Jim and Dave yelling at each other the day before. Mark said, "That's remarkable. Now that I think about it, I haven't noticed them speaking to each other at all."

A few days later, Bob, a friend of both Jim and Dave, asked if he could meet with Mark. When he came in, he apologized for taking his time, but said he was concerned about the relationship between Jim and Dave. A week ago, he had lunch with Jim to discuss the possibilities for a new routing system that he thought would increase efficiency. During their lunch, Bob had mentioned Dave, asking Jim if Dave would be willing to cooperate. Jim burst out, "How the hell do I know what Dave wants? What an idiot! If you want to know what he thinks, ask him!" Jim went on to express his anger at Dave.

Jim's story: *I don't know where Dave is anymore. He won't talk to me. Ever since he broke up with his wife, he's clammed up. When I suggest we do something, he says not to order him around and that he's tired of doing everybody else's work. He says he's interested in having more time for himself and he's not going to spend all his life working anymore. He's got other things to do with his life. I'm not sure his behavior has much to do with his wife. You know, he and I have moved up pretty fast in the last few years and I think it's making his head swim. He never thought he'd get this far. On the other hand, sometimes he acts like he's too good for us. I don't know. Maybe he can't see the big picture—and what the purpose of all this is. Mostly when I see him, I just get angry and say, "Go to hell." It's interfering with my work though because I haven't anybody to talk things through with—and I'm sending my reports straight through the system instead of meeting with Jim. Something's really wrong with that guy.*

After describing his conversation with Jim, Bob said that that was only part of the story. Bob thought maybe Jim was just having a bad day—but then maybe something *was* wrong with Dave. So Bob called Dave up and the two men had lunch. Dave looked fine, not tired or strung out, and seemed to be in good spirits. He was driving a new car and was glad to see Bob. They talked about football for a while. Then Bob asked him how he and Jim were getting along. Dave said calmly, "Jim? Oh, he's fine." When I encouraged him to talk a little more, he changed the subject. A few minutes later, however, Jim happened to walk past our table, nodded at me, scowled at Dave, and kept on going. Dave looked downcast. He started talking about Jim.

Dave's story: *That man's an idiot! We've worked together for years and look how he treats me. He walks right by without saying hello. You know, Jim has been different lately. A few months back he took credit for a report we both wrote. The v.p. called Jim up and said, "What a great report!" and Jim didn't say we'd worked on it together. He didn't admit I had anything to do with it. I guess I'm tired of being pushed around by him. Jim thinks he has such big ideas. He's aiming to be a star around here. You know, when the next promotion comes through at headquarters, there's only one place—instead of the two we have now. I should have that promotion but Jim will get it instead. That's OK, you know. Let him devote his life to the company. Me, I want to enjoy life a little. And I'm not going to work with an S.O.B. that takes credit for everything I do. You know, the other day, Jim drives all the way over to my office, comes inside, asks me a few questions, and then starts yelling at me. Hell, I've got too much living to do to spend my time being yelled at by guys who only think of getting ahead. I'm going to enjoy myself."*

Bob said, "Now, Mark, you know both of them. What can we do. Work's slowing down around here. Today, some of Jim's men refused to talk to Dave's crew. Just now I heard several of them say they were going to send all their work right on to headquarters instead of routing it through Dave's office like they usually do. When I talked to Jim last week, I wanted to make this system better! But, it seems it's getting worse instead."

Mark called Dave's manager and asked him to come to a meeting with both Jim and Dave. Mark was aware his options were limited. Due to economic retrenchment, all promotions and transfers were on hold for an unspecified period of time. Further, the procedure for actually terminating employment for individuals without a long record of incompetence was very lengthy and complicated. Unless the problem was of huge proportions, he knew both men should stay where they were now.

As the meeting opens, Mark is aware of Jim's anger. Jim sits in his chair, banging his pen against the edge. Dave, on the other hand, appears slightly detached but calm. Dave is smiling slightly. What does Mark do now?

CLARIFYING PROBLEMS AND GENERATING ALTERNATIVES

What is the surface nature of the problem?

What are the probable causes?

127

What would be the desired outcome?

What are alternative routes to achieving the desired outcome?

Now use the same questions to clarify problems that currently exist in your organization, develop strategies to resolve areas of difficulty, and then evaluate these strategies.

EVALUATING ALTERNATIVE STRATEGIES

Analyze each strategy you are considering. Use a separate sheet of paper for each strategy and follow this format.

Significance of Outcomes:

Would the expected outcome have effects that will still make a difference in 6 months? 1 year? 2 years?

Would the expected outcome affect only your unit? or other units as well?

Would the expected outcome result in increased resources for the unit in 6 months? 1 year? 2 years?

Would the expected outcome result in increased productivity for the unit in 6 months? 1 year? 2 years?

Would the expected outcome result in increased morale for the unit in 6 months? 1 year? 2 years?

Could any increases in resources, productivity, or morale be negated by other effects either inside or outside your own unit? If yes, detail what these other effects might be.

Overall, summarize the benefits that would result for your unit if the plan were implemented.

Feasibility of Implementation:

Are the resources necessary for implementation available within your unit? Outside your unit? Unavailable?

Are the persons who control the resources identified? Are these individuals likely to give approval to your project?

Have you identified other persons whose approval is necessary in order to implement your plan? Are these individuals likely to give their approval to your project?

Have you identified all individuals who will be affected by implementation of this plan? Have you decided how and when they will be informed of this project? Have you decided to what degree their acceptance of the plan is necessary for successful implementation?

What other possibilities might interfere with the implementation of your plan? Have you prepared contingencies for these possibilities?

Overall, summarize the likelihood of implementing this particular plan.

Shaping
Organizational Change:
The Past, the Present,
and the Future

One department in a large division of a manufacturing concern began to change and people worked more enthusiastically and energetically than they had in years. They believed that they were making the organization as a whole more effective. But as time went on, they perceived that other departments were not following suit but rather were moving as slowly as before, with no repercussions. The department began to taper off it its own efforts. "Why bother?" the employees said to each other.

A manager in a different company straightened out his supply of parts so that he had an even workflow throughout the week. His people were pleased. Within two weeks, however, he was receiving angry memos from the managers of other departments. "Why are you messing up our schedules?" they wanted to know. The new and more efficient schedule initiated by the first manager had disrupted the familiar, if inefficient, schedules of other departments. Each of these examples shows that any change does not occur in isolation but affects the system as a whole.

In this way an organizational system is like a fishnet. A system may be large or small, but in each case it is composed of many interrelated focal points, as knots are interwoven in a net. When any one focal point is changed—moved in one direction or another—it affects all the other focal points in the interrelated system, just as moving any knot in the fishnet changes the shape of the whole. Consequently, prospective changes must be examined in terms of their effect on the entire system. Moreover, each part of a system has a specific history that led it to its present state. Further, each component has future possibilities that can only be hypothesized in the present. As the change process moves along its own time line, it affects things shaped by the past and, in turn, shapes the course of the future. Change, therefore, not only affects all of the system in the present but redirects the course of that system as it moves from the past to the|future (see Figure 9.1).

Difficulties in the Change Process

Many of the difficulties that occur in the change process happen because all situations within a system are interrelated. Some of the problems that may be encountered are due to difficulties within the unit initiating change. Some are due to difficulties external to the unit itself.

Problems internal to the unit may occur. Some of these problems may be symbolized by the threads of a knot in the fishnet simply letting go—so that the knot is loosened and all connecting threads come apart. There are several reasons why this may happen, causing a project to die before it begins. Most of these reasons stem from a *lack of belief* in the outcome and therefore a *lack of commitment* to the process. When tentative beliefs and commitments are challenged by being put to work, people will often give up and give in. Other difficulties may kill a project along the way. A *lack of energy* on the part of some individuals may lead to the dwindling away of the project in the planning stage, as they drift away from the focus of change. Finally, a *lack of vigilance* in monitoring the process may lead to many other people following parallel paths, duplicating efforts, so that the final result is smaller and of less significance to the system. The attentiveness required for coordination of effort has not been brought to bear on the project (see Figure 9.2).

Other reasons are *external*, but can be overcome if sufficient belief, energy, and vigilance are available in the individuals initiating change. However, if there is a lack of any of these characteristics,

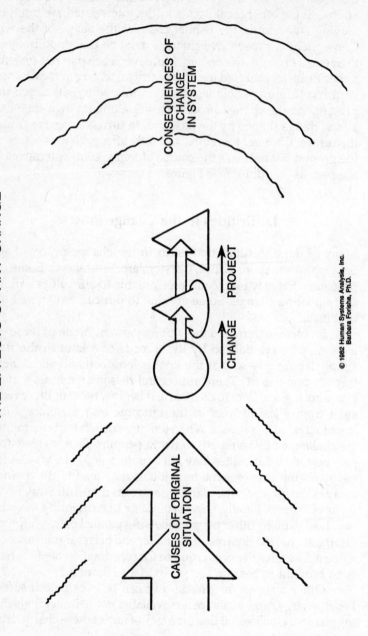

FIGURE 9.1
THE EFFECTS OF ANY CHANGE

CONSEQUENCES OF CHANGE IN SYSTEM

PROJECT

CHANGE

CAUSES OF ORIGINAL SITUATION

© 1982 Human Systems Analysis, Inc.
Barbara Forisha, Ph.D.

FIGURE 9.2
PROBLEMS ENCOUNTERED IN THE CHANGE PROCESS

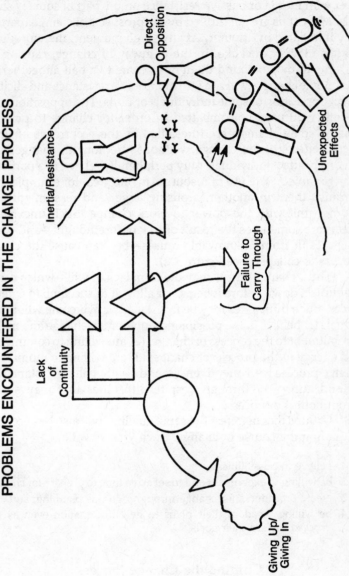

Direct
Opposition

Inertia/Resistance

Lack
of
Continuity

Failure to
Carry Through

Giving Up/
Giving In

Unexpected
Effects

the change project may fade away in the face of external factors. External difficulties may take several forms. Almost all change will meet with inertia or passive resistance on the part of some individuals. Most of us are not thrilled by the prospects of change, particularly if initiated by another. At any given moment, therefore, individuals may sit, rocklike, in the pathway of change, causing the currents to move around them or to come to a halt altogether.

Some changes will run into more active resistance and elicit the direct opposition of some individuals or units. The opposition must be either diffused or combatted in order for change to proceed. Finally, some changes are forestalled by the occurrence of unexpected effects of the change. Without forethought, changes may adversely affect individuals only peripherally related to a particular change project. The use of resources in one area, for example, may diminish them in another, arousing anger and resentment from another unit with the power to block change. Such unexpected effects are sometimes the result of lack of forethought—and sometimes result from unknowable causes—but can cause the change process to collapse (see Figure 9.2).

Thus, change efforts may die from lack of will—which can let the project down before it begins or allow it to succumb to external forces. Such difficulties may be forestalled or overcome when individuals (1) believe in the possibilities inherent in change and make a commitment to the process of change; (2) are willing to commit time and energy to the process of change; (3) are willing to monitor the change process with attentiveness; and (4) are willing to stand their ground and carry through despite difficulties that may surface throughout the process.

Groups that manifest the same qualities will also be successful in guiding the course of change. Such groups will:

1. believe in possibilities;
2. be willing to experiment and to set aside time to prepare for change;
3. create procedures for change through rigorous planning; and
4. be willing to adapt their plans to new information even as they proceed toward their goals.

Guiding the Change Process

There are a number of conclusions to be drawn from this exploration of the process of change. First, organizations that are proving effective in turbulent times are those that seek a balance between pyramidal and circular structures. Second, this search for balance requires individuals to work together as teams in an effort to create new organizational patterns that are effective in these times. Third, in the process of change, new leadership will emerge among those individuals who are willing to evaluate themselves and their organizations, to give up that which is no longer functional, and to create new systems that are responsive to current circumstances. And, fourth, the leaders who emerge will call forth from others the best that they have to offer, so that effective groups will take the leadership in organizations.

The outcome of this process will be more flexible and resilient organizations, that are able to utilize the strengths of all personality styles, match the appropriate structures to each task, and remain responsive to the needs of a changing environment. Yet, as we live through a time of turbulence, we had best draw our rewards from the process, because the outcome, though likely, is not guaranteed. And the outcome, in fact, is to become comfortable with the process of change, which is, in itself, perhaps the most likely outcome.

EXERCISE: ACTION AND IMPLEMENTATION

If you have arrived at some things you would like to change in your organization, you may want to draw up an action plan. Often, managing change requires that individuals persuade others to join with them in this effort. Consequently, they may often need to present their ideas to others in order to win their support. A model for such presentations follows, which you may choose to use in order to prepare a presentation or to clarify for yourself the goals and purposes, the significance and feasibility of your project. The last part presents a model for reviewing, after a period of time, any action you have undertaken. It also provides some useful reminders for areas to be particularly aware of as you manage the process of change.

PRESENTATION FORMAT

1. Identification of goal
   a. Nature of problem
   b. Specific plan of action

2. What steps will have been accomplished in the next five weeks?
What are the short-term costs, if any?
What are the short-term benefits?
3. What steps will have been accomplished in the next six months?
What are the long-term costs, if any?
What are the long-term benefits?
4. What do you see as the overall significance or importance of implementing this project? For your unit? For your division? For the corporation?

PROJECT ACTION PLAN CHECKLIST

On completing your action plan, be sure your plan includes all the following checkpoints. If it does not, you may want to return to your plan and revise the steps to cover all possibilities.

1. Includes acquisition of all necessary resources
2. Includes securing approval from all individuals who have power to veto plan
3. Includes informing all individuals whose support will facilitate implementation of plan
4. Breaks down steps into *measurable* components
5. Assigns *one* person responsibility for each step
6. Shares responsibility for all the steps among more than one or two individuals
7. Establishes realistic timetables for completion of each step
8. Includes method for assessing completion of each step
9. Provides contingency plans for lack of step completion (including alternative routes)
10. Provides recognition (and/or rewards) for step completion
11. Provides opportunities for monitoring progress and redefining steps as necessary
12. Provides opportunities for evaluation of project by all involved

© 1982 Human Systems Analysis, Inc.

ANALYSIS OF COMPLETED PROJECTS

1. Original goal and brief statement of plan:
2. Steps accomplished and comparison with original goal:
3. Areas of greatest success (steps of action plan, particular project areas or specific individual efforts):
4. Areas of least success:

5. Most likely causes of lack of success (internal factors such as lack of time, energy, and commitment or external factors such as inertia, resistance, or opposition):
6. Benefits developing from involvement in project:
7. Liabilities incurred in development of project:
8. Modifications planned for future project involvement:
9. Most significant learnings from involvement in project:

10

The Individual and the Organization: Change, Stress, and Personal Growth

by
Glenn Morris
Consulting Professor, Dow Conference Center, Hillsdale College

Randy Kovach
Senior Associate, Human Systems Analysis, Inc.

Barbara Forisha-Kovach

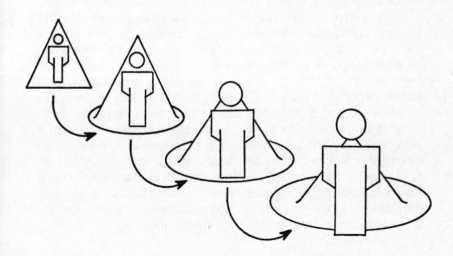

We are all coping with change all the time. Change is occurring on cultural, economic, and social levels. All organizations—and all managers—are responding to the forces of change. Change is often viewed as stress. When change occurs, old boundaries must shift and new ones must be formed. As organizations shift their boundaries, individuals must change their own personal boundaries. How individuals respond to this imperative to change will determine the individual's potential for illness or for health, for psychological retreat or personal growth. The tension an individual experiences between self and organization can create chronic conflict and distress or can motivate a person to change the environment in a beneficial way. The tension between expectations and reality can prompt a person to assume a leadership role in guiding the process of change. In the rest of this chapter, we shall review the forces that are creating change in organizations, the way that individuals may profitably respond to such change, and the new imperative for leadership that is emerging in these times of change.

Cultural Change

The world looks very different now than it did ten years ago—at least to most individuals in organizations. Countries have drawn closer together and form one global commercial network in which the international marketplace has superseded national and regional territories. At the same time, within highly industrialized cultures, the growth in technology has transformed the internal workings of business operations. Not only must managers respond to a new big picture on the international scene but a new "little picture"—the details of many new technical operations. In each area, organizational boundaries have shifted, and personal boundaries must shift as well. The new demands produce tension within individuals and that tension may be used for either good or ill.

Managers today must know much more than managers some years ago. They must have knowledge about the markets and the peoples of other countries. They must also have an understanding of the technological capabilities of new machines within the company. No one person can master all the required knowledge. A manager needs input from other people about the large world and the small one. What one person used to do now takes two or more. Consequently, management is becoming even more of a team effort than it has in the past. And individuals must learn to work in teams and to communicate well with each other in order to make the teams effective. The changes in the demand for knowledge in the last several years lead, therefore, to changes in the demand for interpersonal skills. Individual managers must adapt not only to new cultural and technological demands but also to new demands on their interpersonal abilities. These demands would certainly be expected to create tension between individuals and their organizations, and this tension may sometimes be termed stress.

Individual Response to Change

Stress may be viewed as change. Since everything changes over time, just being alive creates stress. Stress is a natural fact of life for all of us. Anything that happens in our lives has the potential for being stressful. Things that cause stress are called *stressors*. It is not the event or the stressor itself, however, which causes stress, but how we react to it. How we think determines whether or not we experience stress. Which strategies we choose to respond to change have an effect on whether or not we experience stress. Stress is the response we make to events and is reflected in our well-being, our physical, mental and emotional states.

Contrary to popular belief, stress can be regarded in two ways. Stress may be regarded in a negative sense as *distress*, or anxiety. Distress is wear and tear on the mind and body. Then, stress may be regarded as *eustress*, or excitement and exhilaration. Eustress is growth and satisfaction. How one responds to change determines whether one will experience distress or eustress.

Consider the life events you may have experienced during the past two years. Suppose a child left home, you transferred to a new community, got a divorce, or had trouble with in-laws. How you think about these events, how you respond to them, will determine your level of stress. There is some evidence that the more events like this that you experience, the more likely you are to experience some form of psychosomatic illness. There is other evidence, however, that the frequency of significant life events may not, in and of itself, produce medical symptoms. For some people, a higher frequency of changeful events is significantly associated with *lower* frequency of psychosomatic or medical symptoms. For individuals who are committed to finding long-term solutions to their problems and who are willing to work at it, a higher number of changeful events simply provides more challenges and could be said to result in another form of stress—eustress. Such individuals not only have low levels of stress-related medical symptoms, but also understand practices of good management, interpersonal relationships, learning and reasoning processes, planning, problem solving, and decision making.

When you are confronted with change and/or the necessity of making changes in your life, the willingness to take action, to commit yourself to something that is meaningful, is an essential component in preventing illness. The opportunity to act in the face of change contributes to physical and emotional well-being. Yet we all have that opportunity to take control of our lives by determining the ways in which we respond to change. Let us look now at some

144

personality characteristics that modify the ways in which individuals can respond to change to turn distress into eustress.

1. Willingness to share your life experience with others acts as a buffer to stress in a number of ways. Sharing with others engenders acceptance and trust. Not only does one have the support of friends, but through sharing experiences, one acquires a greater understanding of a variety of experiences. In other words, one becomes more sophisticated, consequently reducing egocentrism and a tendency to see the world from only one point of view. Further, trusting others tends to create environments in which others grow more trusting. Consequently, sharing experiences with others has often been related to emotional stability, positive assertion, and even creativity. The individual who is willing to share with others exhibits strength of character, warmth, and sincerity.

2. An individual who is open to new experiences will increase the probability that change will be accepted without fear. The person who is more open to new ideas is more likely to recognize the need for change, as well as to instigate change.

3. The ability to solve problems also tends to lower stress or turn distress into eustress. Good analytical skills are at the root of problem solving. Analytical skills prevent people from jumping to incorrect conclusions or selecting inappropriate solutions. People with an analytical bent are more likely to figure out what the real source of a problem is and to select the solution that works to alleviate the problem.

4. In a complex modern society the ability to think in terms of complete systems and their interfaces definitely relates to the ability to solve problems. Seeing the complete system means that patterns of relationship are revealed. One sees the big picture. A person who does this is able to integrate knowledge from a wide variety of sources. Skills in pattern recognition and integration allow a person to better predict what may happen and interpret what is happening. This is a valuable asset when dealing with change.

5. The ability to make decisions and live with the responsibility for those decisions is a buffer against anxiety. Harry Truman's famous motto "The buck stops here" exemplifies this attitude. A person high on decision-making skills will consider alternatives and evaluate their probable effects before choosing a plan of action. The decision maker who is willing to withhold judgment, evaluate alternatives on their merits, and take responsibility without placing blame is likely to make final decisions on the best possible information. Such a person is less likely to leap into situations with unexpected and unhappy consequences and less likely to experience the negative effects of change.

6. Finally, individuals who are willing to act and to accomplish their own objectives—despite obstacles—show markedly fewer signs of stress than do other people. Such individuals are often able to accomplish multiple tasks and enjoy stretching themselves. They often move on and create change if none is forthcoming without their initiative because, to them, change presents a challenge.

As we live in this time of tremendous social and economic change, we are all responsible for how we view this age of transition. Each individual has a responsibility to use the tension resulting from change to enlarge his or her own world and that of others. Specifically, within organizations, if individuals recognize and accept the tension that may exist between their own expectations and those of their organization, they can use this discrepancy as motivation for both personal growth and organizational change.

Individuals and Organizations

Individuals in organizations in changing times experience every degree of tension with their organization. Some individuals—those who adapt relatively well to change—are right in sync with their organization and demonstrate relatively little tension or stress. The pace of organizational change is right in step with their own personal pace of change. Other individuals are moderately or extremely out of sync with their organizations. These individuals fall into two categories.

First are those individuals who are ahead of their organizations in terms of desire for and adaptability to change. These individuals often experience lots of change in their personal lives and thrive on challenges. They may feel restricted by their organization and impatient for it to catch up. They are often in the forefront in terms of

146

urging that organizational members learn better communication skills and open up to each other.

Second are those individuals who are behind their organizations in terms of desire for and adaptability to change. These individuals feel as if changes are moving too quickly for them, leaving them without guidelines—in limbo. They demand of their organizations that they temper the rush toward change by establishing rules, procedures, and guidelines for times of transition, and that caution be exercised in attempting the new or sidelining the old.

All three groups of individuals are necessary in successfully guiding the process of organizational change. Those who experience the least tension around the change process may emerge as central leaders of the organization, shaping and monitoring the integration of new and old programs. Those who experience tension because they believe the organization does not move quickly enough, will champion new programs, create new procedures, and insist on training and development needs to help promote organizational change. Those who experience tension because they believe that the organization is moving too quickly will argue for caution, will scrutinize new programs, and insist that rules and procedures be developed to channel the course of change. Each of these groups of individuals provides a balance for the others, as organizations come to terms with the new realities of a changing world.

That is, each of these groups will provide a balance for others *if they choose to do so*. Individuals who sit back in the face of disparity between personal and organizational expectations, hoping that the organization will do something for them, often experience the negative effects of tension. They are those who will experience stress as distress. Individuals who act to decrease the tension through both personal and organizational change, and who are doing something for the organization, often experience the positive effects of tension. They experience stress as eustress—as challenge and excitement. Because their response to change is positive and constructive, they place themselves in control of the process of change (see Example 10.1).

Individuals who experience tension and act to create change are informal change agents within organizations. Such individuals distinguish themselves by their skill in communication and their ability to work with a group of people. Because they listen well, they understand the other person's point of view. Because they know themselves, they are also able to communicate clearly their own point of view. Such individuals become centers of influence within organizations. Depending on their own degree of fit with the organization, these change agents may urge organizations to open up communication channels, to develop clear guidelines for the time of transition, or they may become spokespersons for the central organizational direction. In all cases, their ability to guide change and their influence rests on their ability to communicate and work with others. Out of these characteristics comes their leadership potential.

Example 10.1 Tension and Change Capability

John Paulson is in sync with his organization. He works for a large company moving toward participative management, which he perceives to be a balance of pyramids and circles. He, himself, is an Integrator and comfortable with this balance. As the organization has moved to create change within itself, Mr. Paulson has assumed a formal leadership role in guiding that process. He is pleased with the pace of change for it suits his own.

Tom Hanover is out of sync with his organization and experiences tension between his own expectations and those of his organization. He agrees with others that his organization is becoming more circular and that communication and teamwork are receiving new emphasis. Mr. Hanover, himself, however, prefers to focus on getting the work done and views much of this new emphasis as "crap." For a while, he became bitter about the direction of his organization and retreated into his own work area and focused solely on his job. As time went on, however, he was drawn into a number of planning meetings and has become an important influence in making sure that new procedures and systems are carefully thought through and understood before implementation. Mr. Hanover is a Producer in a conical environment.

Arnie Matthews is also out of sync with his organization and often feels frustrated by the lack of change in the organization. His perception is not shared by either John Paulson or Tom Hanover, who work for the same company. Mr. Matthews, however, is always on the go, wandering around talking to people, and creating new ideas for product lines. He, himself, likes change and is impatient for his organization to catch up. In recent times, he has become influential in getting new training programs begun in the organization and opening up channels of communication between subordinates and their boss. Rather like a gadfly, he is continually reminding the others that they cannot be complacent with the changes that have occurred already—for there are more to come. Mr. Matthews is a Processor.

The Leadership Imperative

If we are to survive in the next years, it is incumbent upon all of us to develop our leadership potential and to take control of the process of change. Organizations that survive and prosper will have within them many individuals who have become centers of influence and who focus attention on the need for continuity as well as the need for change. Organizations that fail to survive and/or prosper will have within them many individuals who have given up their influence to others and wait for somebody to do something for them. Such individuals are at the mercy of their environments—and allow themselves to be victims of the change process.

In order to increase our own leadership potential, we need to strengthen our abilities to work well with others. We need to know our own mind—and how to speak it—and also know when to be silent and listen to others. When we do both of these things, we will then have the information on ourselves and our environment that will help us to make the best decisions in any given situation. We will have the fullest array of facts and opinions from our associates, as well as an understanding of our own point of view, and on that basis will be able to responsibly make decisions and accept the consequences. Anyone who does so is a leader within his or her group.

Tension *is* beneficial. Many of us would sit in the sun all day doing little else if our environments suited us in all particulars. Because this is often not the case, we get up and do something. Because our organizational environment differs from how we think it could be, many of us are actively involved in the change process. We cannot simply sit in the sun and expect others to make things better without our own participation. We must utilize the tension to improve our communication, better our teamwork, and act so as to bring our environments more in line with our expectations. To the extent that all of us develop our own potential we will use the changes in our lives to create eustress and not distress and will move toward taking leadership in this time of change.

What this means in terms of the theme of this book is that as organizations move toward an integration of pyramids and circles, individuals themselves will have to grow in order to profit from this integration. Producers must grow to the level at which they are at home in team settings and make the most of their potential for positive team contributions. Integrators must use their talents to help others to achieve rather than focusing on their own achievement. They must use this opportunity to create the systems and the procedures that provide some stability in times of change. Processors, finally, must stop talking and start doing something, often showing others the direction in which change will move. All Producers, Integrators, and Processors, in fact, who choose the path of personal growth (rather than retreat) will use their own tensions in the face of change to create better organizations that balance caution and innovation, consistency and flexibility, continuity and change, and that weave into the organizational fabric a new balance between pyramids and circles.

EXERCISE: YOU, BELIEF SYSTEMS, AND CHANGE CAPABILITY

Follow the directions below in order to estimate your degree of tension with your organization, the direction of that tension, and your capacity to enact change in your environment.

Belief Systems

Organizational.   To find the *degree of tension* that you experience around the issues of organizational change, subtract your average score on the MINI-PXI (pp. 37–39) from your average score on the MINI-OXI (pp. 23–25). If the resulting number falls between +2 and −2, you experience only a moderate degree of tension about change. If the number is greater than +2 or less than −2, you experience a correspondingly greater degree of tension around the issues of organizational change.

   To find the *direction* in which you think the organization should move in order to minimize your tension, notice the + or − sign preceding the number indicating degree of tension. Interpret this in the following manner:

   A + sign indicates that you believe the organization would become more effective if everyone knew what the expectations of the organization were at this time and if the rules and procedures of the organization were applied consistently across the board. Individuals who have a high degree of tension preceded by a + may either (1) believe that their organization is moving too quickly in a participative direction and that more caution and some return to the "old ways" of management is necessary; or (2) agree with new participative trends in their organization but believe that more rules and regulations, consistently applied, should accompany the transition to prevent individuals from feeling as if they are operating in limbo; or (3) believe that their organization is basically spineless and unable to develop coherent policies with which to transact business.

A − sign indicates that you believe the organization would become more effective if individuals learned to communicate better, develop more effective teams, and in general pay more attention to individuals within the organization. Some individuals with a high degree of tension around change and a − preceding the tension number may be impatient for new worlds that they can envision but are far from being enacted in most organizational settings.

Group. To find the *degree of tension* that you experience in interaction with your immediate work group subtract your average score on the MINI-PXI (pp. 37–39) from your average score on the MINI-GPI (pp. 71–73). If the resulting number falls between +2 and −2, you experience only a moderate degree of tension in interaction with your work group. If the number is greater than +2 or less than −2, you experience a correspondingly greater degree of tension in interaction with your work group.

To find the *direction* in which you believe you or your work group should move in order to minimize this tension, notice the + or − sign preceding the number indicating degree of tension. Interpret this in the following manner:

A + sign indicates that you believe your group is more open to change than you yourself are. It may mean that you are hurrying to catch up with your group and that they, in fact, are leading the way into a more open style of management. On the other hand, you may believe that your group is wild and unruly and that they would be better served by a more conscientious attention to organizational rules, procedures, and expectations.

A − sign indicates that you believe your group would profit from improving their communication and teamwork skills. You, yourself, are probably more open to change than they and are impatient for them to catch up. Sometimes these scores indicate that you would like your group to be more open *with you* and may wonder, in fact, why they do not share as much of their experience with you as you would like.

Change Capability

Use your change capability score (pp. 90–91) to determine how you respond to the degree of tension which you experience in your organization or with your work group. Use the chart below to determine your probable response to varying degrees of tension according to the degree of change capability.

Change Capability	Degree of Tension	
	Moderate	*High*
Low	You are probably relatively content with the current state of affairs in your organization or your group. In general, expectations of your behavior are set by others, but they accord with what you would like for yourself and you experience little need to change things.	You are probably experiencing considerable stress with your organization and/or work group and feel powerless to change things. You may feel somewhat like a victim in your current organizational setting.
Moderate	You are probably relatively content with the current state of affairs in your or- ganization or your group. In some areas, you have assisted in establishing expectations for your behavior and that of others and believe that your efforts make some difference, but in other areas you accept things the way they are whether you like them or not.	You are probably experiencing considerable tension between your organization and/or work group and yourself and, in some areas, are actively trying to change things to fit your own belief system. In some areas, however, you feel you can do little to affect change and are sometimes resentful and/or bewildered by the way these areas operate.

High

You are probably relatively content with the current state of affairs in your organization or your group. The reason you are pleased is that you have had a large hand in shaping the expectations that govern your environment. If you believe something is not operating in the best way possible, you act so as to improve the situation. In most situations, you find yourself feeling "at home," since you are a strong influence on designing these situations and they are often created to fit your own beliefs and expectations.

You are probably experiencing considerable tension between your organization, your work group, and/or yourself, but you are enjoying the challenges that this tension provides and enthusiastic about the opportunities for changing things in ways you believe will be more effective. It is not likely that you will remain in this environment for long without diminishing the tension between you and the organization, for you will bring others along your own path.

Direction of Change

Combine your interpretative summaries for the *direction* of change with those given under change *capability* to have an estimate of the areas in which you experience the most stress or are making the greatest change efforts. It is clear to us that stress and change efforts are usually mutually exclusive. If we experience stress because of disparities between ourselves and our environment, we are often brooding about the differences rather than acting to make them less. If we are working for change, on the other hand, we are often motivated and exhilarated by the discrepancies between our expectations and those of others and are, by our own efforts, likely to diminish these discrepancies.

Index